The Ultimate Lesson
10 POINT GUIDE
ON HOW TO TEACH YOURSELF ANYTHING

By Art Niemann

SLI Press, Los Angeles, California

The Ultimate Lesson
10 POINT GUIDE
ON HOW TO TEACH YOURSELF ANYTHING
by Art Niemann

Published by:
SLI Press
Niemann Enterprises, Inc.
16161 Ventura Blvd., #C-753
Los Angeles, California 91436
http://www.selflearn.com

This publication is designed to provide accurate and authoritative information in regard to the subject matter covered. It is sold with the understanding that the publisher is not engaged in rendering legal, accounting, or other professional services. If legal advice or other expert assistance is required, the services of a competent professional person should be sought.

The purpose of this book is to educate, inform, and entertain. The author and publisher shall have neither liability nor responsibility to any person or entity with respect to any loss or damage caused, or alleged to be caused, directly or indirectly by the information contained in this book.

Printed in the United States of America
First Printing April 1996

10 9 8 7 6 5 4 3 2 1

ISBN: 0-9651335-5-9
$14.95 softcover

Library of Congress Catalog Card Number: 96-92211

Publisher's Cataloging in Publication Data
Niemann, Art
The Ultimate Lesson: 10 Point Guide on How to Teach Yourself Anything
1. Self Education I. Title
2. Self Help
3. Success in Business
4. Business
5. Management
6. Entrepreneurship

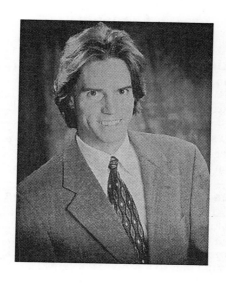

About the Author

Born and raised in Boston, Art Niemann is a self-taught entrepreneur who began his self-learning odyssey at an early age. He taught himself piano at age five, started a business at age nine, and began programming computers at age fourteen.

A four-year Air Force tour saw him travel throughout Europe as a reporter and producer for the Armed Forces Radio and Television Service. More recently, he set up a recording studio and produced the debut album from his band, Veronica's Toy, in which he is also the keyboard player. He resides in Los Angeles.

Contents

1. Unlocking the World **1**
    The Importance of Teaching Yourself 3
    People Who Learn On Their Own 6
    The Pros and Cons of Traditional Learning 10
    Limits 10

2. The First Lesson **13**
    Learning to Walk 13
    You Can Teach Yourself 14
    The Piano and the Wastebasket 15

3. The Ten Points of The Ultimate Lesson **21**
    1. Find the Incentive 21
    2. Enforce the Belief 22
    3. Follow Your Own Guidance 22
    4. Begin with Small Steps 23
    5. Learn From Your Mistakes 23
    6. Use Patterns 24
    7. Adapt to the Requirements 24
    8. Overcome the Obstacles 24
    9. Fill in the Gaps 24
    10. Judge the Results 25
    Overview 25

4. Find the Incentive **27**
    Goal-Setting 27
    Motivation 40
    Conclusion 45

5. Enforce the Belief **47**
    Belief and Fear is Learned Behavior 47
    Learning and Unlearning Beliefs and Fears 55

6. Follow Your Own Guidance **61**
    Keep the End Result in Mind 61
    Supporting Materials 66
    Staying On Course 71
    Make Corrections 72
    Watch the Winners 74

7. Begin With Small Steps **79**
    We Learn By Doing 79
    Build Confidence: Take Your First Small Step 82
    Pacing Yourself 85

8. Learn From Your Mistakes 89
  Trial and Error 89
9. Use Patterns 97
  Recognizing Patterns 97
  Transposing a Pattern 100
10. Adapt to the Requirements 103
  Conditioning Your Mind and Body 103
  Allowing Yourself to Adapt 106
11. Overcome the Obstacles 109
  Intellectual Obstacles 109
  Physical Obstacles 116
12. Fill in the Gaps 121
  Identify What Is Missing 121
13. Judge the Results 125
  The Judgment System 125
14. Ten-Point Review 131
  Let the Ten Points Work Together 141
15. Applying Your Ability 143
  Learning a New Skill 143
  Advancing at Work 146
  Building a Business 150
  Productive Play 154
  From Parent to Child 155
  In Times of Crisis 156
16. The Future of Traditional Education 161
  Affordable Education is Coming 161
17. The Ongoing Challenge 167
  Be a Self-Starter 167
  What Now? 168
Epilogue: Two Self-Learning Adventures 171
  The Ultimate Lesson: The Book 171
  Veronica's Toy: The Debut Album 174
  Finished Products 176
  What's Next For Me? 177
Acknowledgments 179

Give someone a fish and they eat for a day.

Teach them to fish and they eat for a lifetime...

Or until they tire of fish.

1 Unlocking the World

At one time or another we've all faced a challenge or task that we thought we just couldn't handle. What would you say if someone who had little or no training or education in a particular subject stepped in and quickly figured it out completely on her own? You would take a step back, shake your head, and wonder how she did it. Helen hadn't tackled anything like this before; She'd had no formal training, she didn't follow a detailed set of instructions, and she didn't wait around for somebody else to show her what to do. If you weren't envious, you might compliment her by saying, "Helen, you're pretty good at that. You must have a knack for it."

Imagine that a few weeks later you run into Helen again. This time you might find her expressing herself

1

creatively by painting some beautiful picture. You are amazed. You might suspect that she had studied art for many years to be able to paint like that, but when you ask Helen where she learned her skill, she says she never studied formally. "I enjoy painting and just paint what I see and feel."

Would it be correct to say that Helen has a knack for painting? Certainly, but if you were to give her another challenge that she desired to take on, she'd probably teach herself whatever she needed to know in order to meet that challenge as well.

Imagine if you had the ability to teach yourself anything. If you could do that, chances are that most of the barriers that presently hold you back would vanish. Well, I have some good news for you! Self-learning is not some skill reserved only for "geniuses," nor does it have language or cultural barriers. It is a skill that we all share, regardless of race, sex, age, upbringing, wealth, or anything else you believe limits your potential.

The Ultimate Lesson will show you how you can master anything that you want to learn, naturally and effortlessly. Once you discover how to teach yourself, your life will have virtually no limits. All the world's teachers and trainers combined cannot teach you a fraction of what you can teach yourself.

The Ultimate Lesson does not give you something you don't already have. Instead, it enables you to realize the amazing ability you are unaware that you already possess. As you progress through this book, you will see a lot of conventional "wisdom" go right out the window.

At the same time, you will understand that you are sitting on top of a gold mine of personal power and ability, just waiting for you to tap into it.

The Importance of Teaching Yourself

Many of life's challenges can bring us substantial rewards if we merely undertake them. Unfortunately, there are very few Ann Sullivans (Helen Keller's teacher) to take a passionate interest in helping us realize our potential.

Traditional teachers are paid to share their knowledge, whether or not their instruction yields results. Therefore, they have little incentive to ensure that their students will benefit from the knowledge. On the other hand, a teacher who had the proper motivation would make sure you were well taught. He would make sure you understood and followed through on everything, thereby benefiting from the knowledge. He can only be properly motivated if he has a significant stake in your growth and well-being. Who holds a greater stake, who has more potential motivation to teach you, than you yourself?

Throughout this learning process you are going to wear two hats, one as a student and one as your own teacher. Your growth is the reward for a job well done, so naturally you will do a much more effective job of teaching yourself than could ten professors who don't share the same powerful incentive. Chances are you've done this already, perhaps when you saw something you wanted to try and then tried it. If you think it might be fun to learn to play tennis, but have nobody to teach you, you can take a few trips to the neighborhood tennis courts to learn the rules of the game. You'll see that you need a tennis racquet, some fuzzy white or yellow balls, and some persistence. Procure the equipment and practice hitting the balls against the wall. After you've hit a thousand of them, the stroke of the racquet will begin to feel more natural. Find someone to practice with, sign up for a court, and play. If you enjoy it, you might decide to play regularly, and over time you will develop skills and proficiency in different parts of your game. The forehand stroke, the backhand stroke, the serve, the volley, and the overhead smash will start feeling more natural, and your stroke will become consistently more powerful with time and practice.

You'll feel great personal satisfaction when you learn something on your own. Self-learning can help you advance professionally and socially, you can learn at your own pace, and it's fun. You can choose to learn over a long period of time or blast through your course of study ten times faster than if you were locked in a typical classroom environment. You won't be held back by the structured pace of a class with students who have varying degrees of ability.

Don't Get Left Behind

In the days when a college education was followed by a lifetime career, a student would graduate from a university or trade school between the ages of 22 and 25, then devote his working career to a company until retirement.

Today companies come and go overnight and entire industries can become obsolete in a very short time. In the last one hundred years the transportation industry has evolved from horses and stagecoaches to cars, trains, and planes. Fifty years ago the computer was a vacuum-tube prototype that filled a room. Now it is small enough to fit on a desk and is as common as the TV set.

The person who spent only his early years learning and then stopped can end up jobless when his knowledge becomes obsolete. For instance, the technicians and scientists who attended school in the '30s and '40s hoped to be on the forefront of the technological advances that were expected to revolutionize the world in the '50s and '60s. The demand for their knowledge came and went in a blinding flash, and by the early '70s technology had advanced far beyond what most people had imagined. Thousands of highly skilled workers, many of whom made great sacrifices for their knowledge, were rendered obsolete. They assumed their knowledge would be in demand for the rest of their working lifetime, but suddenly, in what they thought would be the prime of their lives, they found they were no longer needed. Many of them went back to school but found they were no match for the younger generation who raced right past them.

Now the industry is changing so fast a significant technical revolution seems to occur almost every five years. A student will not benefit from many years of schooling if he can't use his knowledge productively. Today's business career, and perhaps life as well, requires constant learning and growth. No school in the world can give you enough knowledge to last you the rest of your life. You must learn continually by yourself.

Our world changes so rapidly, nobody is safe from the onslaught of advancement, and those who choose not to adapt will most certainly be left behind. Today's workers can expect to have four to five different jobs or career changes during their working lifetime.

Self-Learning Can Take You Anywhere

Your desire for independence can be a strong motivator. Once you tap into your ability to teach yourself you can adapt to the changes or challenges the world throws at you. The first time you teach yourself something you will gain confidence you might not have imagined you could possess. As a result of your new confidence, you will know that you can learn just about anything, without being dependent on others.

People Who Learn On Their Own

Leaders

The leader of a company knows the value of self-education. He is faced with a myriad of decisions every day, and is responsible for evaluating them and then making the appropriate choices for his company. The right decision can propel his company to new highs, while the wrong decision can send the company tumbling into bankruptcy. The boss has no one to turn to for guidance. Various sources of information can influence his decision, but the burden is his alone, so he cannot afford to be indecisive.

When he makes a decision, nobody will slap his hand and tell him he's wrong, and nobody will jump up and down and tell him what a brilliant move he made. Only the results of his decisions will determine whether he was right or wrong. Chances are, he made good decisions as he was rising through the ranks of the company. He taught himself how to be the boss and subsequently got the top job. Ambitious executives can attend classes to learn to become "leaders," but successful leaders have done a great deal of learning on their own in addition to any formal education or training.

Employees

A company boss has usually spent a significant amount of time as an employee, and knows that valuable employees must be treated well. Self-learners and self-starters have a good chance of being promoted, and a boss who is secure in his position will encourage his employees to learn on their own and try new things. Employees who have the courage to try something new and innovative are frequently rewarded with promotions.

Employees are often much more powerful than they realize. Cathy started out as the shipping and receiving clerk at the XYZ Corporation warehouse. She was very interested in her job, and learned a great deal about the warehouse procedures. She knew where the system bottlenecked, and saw how it could be improved. She discussed her observations with her supervisor, who quickly approved of and implemented Cathy's suggestions. As a result, the warehouse ran more smoothly, and

Cathy was rewarded with a raise and promotion. But Cathy didn't stop there. She kept learning, and continued to discuss her findings with her supervisors. After only a short time with XYZ Corporation, Cathy was promoted to warehouse manager.

Entrepreneurs

A person who starts her own business is a prime example of a self-learner. Much like a company boss, nobody tells a business owner whether her decisions are right or wrong, but the profit-and-loss sheet will tell the story. An entrepreneur should be familiar with the many different aspects of starting a business, running it, and making it successful. Jane may start out with little more than an idea for a product or service that she believes will sell. From ground zero, she learns everything she can about product design, manufacturing, sales, marketing, and finance. She invests time in learning about her business because a good portion of her own money is at stake. If Jane does not learn to produce and sell her product or service effectively, she stands to lose a great deal.

Inventors

Inventors start from scratch, quickly learning by trial and error. They represent the ultimate example of a self-learner.

Let's assume Frank has an idea for a product that does not yet exist. He imagines how the finished product will look and how it will work. He draws a diagram of his product, then he researches methods of assembling materials into a crude prototype. This is just a first guess at what will work, not a plan for a finished product. He thinks it might work, but Frank's first prototype isn't quite right. Frank's job is just beginning. It's not enough to know that it didn't work, he must now find out why it didn't work. When Frank finds out why his prototype didn't work he makes changes based upon what he has learned and tries again. This happens hundreds of times before Frank's invention is ready to be produced and sold.

Students

A student who advances to the top of her class is a self-learner regardless of her age. She is highly motivated and productive, and if she is ever caught doing something without permission it's probably reading ahead in her textbooks. A self-learning student has a tremendous advantage over her counterparts who wait to be told what to learn. A college student who "invents" her own project might deservedly get extra credit.

Children

Children are masters of self-learning. These geniuses have never been told that they cannot do what they envision, or that they cannot learn on their own. If they see something they want to do, they will try it with little or no thought of success or failure. If at first they are not successful they continue to try until they do succeed. Many of us could learn a great deal by watching children in action.

The Pros and Cons of Traditional Learning

Traditional school covers many of the important basics, but it plays a relatively small role in your overall learning experience. A conventional education in all likelihood will not provide you with all the information you'll need to carry you through your working lifetime.

In traditional school, we learn to be dependent upon others to provide us with knowledge. All too often this habit is formed at an early age and stays with us for many years. This dependence can hinder us when we're faced with modern-day challenges in which we must seek knowledge on our own. Furthermore, higher education at universities and colleges is becoming quite costly and is not always readily available to everyone.

By pushing your intelligence to its limits, you'll get all the education you will ever need through non-traditional methods virtually for free.

Limits

You will discover your true limits by learning from your mistakes. The main principle of *The Ultimate Lesson* is to learn by doing. When you experiment without guidance there will be occasions when things go wrong, so you must be reasonably sure that you can live with the worst possible outcome.

It's all right to make mistakes provided nobody is endangered as a result. For instance, how many self-trained lawyers, doctors, or pilots have you heard of? The cost of a mistake while learning such a profession is too high. A single mistake could have fatal consequences. If there is potential danger in what you wish to do and a mistake could be devastating, you must set up a safety net that will "catch you if you fall."

You'll learn more about this later. For now, open your mind and prepare to embark on a stimulating journey of self-discovery.

2 The First Lesson

Learning to Walk

Just about everybody learns to walk. It's one of the first things we learn on our own without instruction manuals or lessons, and it's a prime illustration of successful self-learning.

The lesson begins when a child sees her parents walking. Baby Jody wants to be just like the grown-ups, to go where they go, as quickly as they go, instead of crawling slowly on the floor. After some experimentation with her leg muscles, Jody tries to stand up by herself, but falls down. With a little persistence, she's able to stand upright all by herself. Then she tries to take a step as she's seen her parents do many times. She falls down on the second step, but Jody's desire to walk persists. Up again, down again, she learns how to balance and move her legs. She has a few hard falls and cries a bit, but doesn't give up. When she finally can take a few steps unaided, Jody is rewarded with her family's approval.

When Jody becomes an adult, small failures are more difficult for her to overcome. "I've failed. I'll never try anything again because I can't stand the thought of being humiliated in front of my family and friends." That may be her reaction to failure now, but she probably had no such fear when she was learning to walk.

Such a spectacular "failure" is really just a result of experimentation. To attain success as a child, you modify your approach, try something different, and complete four or five steps before falling down again. If you refuse to believe that what you're attempting to do is "impossible," you won't associate falling down with failure. You may fall a few hundred times before you get it right, but you'll keep getting up and trying again until you produce the results you want. Since you're a child it never occurs to you to quit.

You Can Teach Yourself

If you can walk it proves you have already taught yourself something on your own. Unfortunately, after this all-important and formative lesson, most of us go down an entirely different and less productive path.

Frustration is one of our first emotions. Whether it is an interesting object on the table or his mother's milk, a child doesn't always get what he wants. He has a limited vocabulary, so he tries pointing at the object of his desire, and crying. It works! His parents give him what he wants just to "shut him up." This solves one problem but creates another. An extremely powerful and limiting association is now formed in his subconscious. His brain links up crying and screaming with someone giving him whatever he wants. If every circumstance was like this he might become dependent on others later in life.

On the other hand, if he's alone (Mom and Dad are in the other room) he learns to fend for himself. He wonders what he can play with. In my case it was the TV set. My parents told me I sat on my dad's lap when I was little and watched as he turned it on and changed channels. They frequently found me alone in the living room, fiddling with the TV until I got a picture and sound, switching channels until I liked what I saw.

A combination of good and bad adventures, and successful and unsuccessful experiences, creates a subconscious foundation for our future conduct. Our tremendous learning rate in our first few years of life enables us to enter adulthood with useful knowledge and beliefs based on our early experiences. Learn to organize your experiences and take advantage of them.

The Piano and the Wastebasket

The Piano

I became aware of my own self-learning ability when I was five years old. I clearly remember the day an old upright piano was delivered to our house. I didn't know why we got it until three weeks later when my grandmother came to visit. She knew how to play the piano because she had been a musician and a singer. Thanks to an old songbook that just so happened to be in the piano bench when it arrived, she played Christmas carols while I watched and listened.

I got a bird's-eye view of her hands and fingers as she played. I noticed that her left hand played the bass notes and her right hand played the melody, and I could hear the difference between them. She played every song in the book, hitting the notes with precision as she read from the page. I glanced up at the book a few times, but to me the songs just looked like a bunch of lines, dots and squiggles. Instead of trying to read the songs from the book, I concentrated on her fingers as they moved across the keyboard. As I watched her play the chord progressions and musical notes, I wanted to be able to do it too. After she played the songs a few times, I heard the tunes in my head. I had already enjoyed four Christmas seasons, and was very well acquainted with the song "Jingle Bells." I couldn't have forgotten it if I'd tried.

One afternoon I sat down at the piano to play "Jingle Bells." I reached out with the index finger of my right hand and struck a note. It sounded too high to be the first note of "Jingle Bells" so I struck a lower note. It was too low so I tried pressing each of the keys in between until I hit the right note. Many years later I learned the name of the note: E above middle C. At that moment it just sounded good and that's all that mattered to me. With one note down, I went on to find the next note, using the same process of trial and error. It didn't take as long the second time because I had done it once already. Repeating the process, I located each of the notes that make up the melody of "Jingle Bells." The next step was to play it like a song, with the notes in the right sequence, a one-fingered version of "Jingle Bells." It felt awkward. As I hit each note, I had to think about it and guess whether it was the right note or not. My first attempt at piano playing sounded about as good as hunt-and-peck typing.

My parents got used to hearing the Christmas carols my grandmother played each day from the downstairs room. The shock came a few weeks later when they heard the same music coming from the piano room while my grandmother was upstairs, nowhere near the piano! They ran down to the piano room, and there I was, playing "Jingle Bells" just like Grandma played it, when I'd only been "playing" for a month.

The Wastebasket

The computer room at my junior high school was really nothing more than a closet. It had two terminals that were hooked up to the high school computer by telephone lines. They were old-fashioned teletype machines that slowly printed out information on rolls of paper, dinosaurs by today's standards. The students in the computer class learned computer programming methods on the blackboard in the classroom and then walked down the hall to try the programs on the computer.

The terminals were broken half the time; whether it was vandalism or poor technology, I don't know. Perhaps the students were just banging the keys a little too hard.

As a result, the two terminals were moved into the audio-visual room near the school library where the teachers could keep an eye on them.

I was not in the computer class, but I spent much of my time in the audio-visual room. I watched the computer students try out their programs as the machines churned out endless streams of paper that filled the wastebaskets at the end of the day. There were questions and answers, programs that worked, and programs that failed. The daily batch of useless paper was a full-sized trash load for the custodians to empty at night.

I was bored one day after everyone else had gone home and pulled a piece of paper out of the wastebasket. A simple math program that used variable numbers and performed routine calculations was written on it. It made sense to me. Just to see what would happen, I spent five minutes typing in the program and then typed the word "run." It worked exactly as I thought it would. After running it a couple of times I went back to the program code itself and made a couple of changes just to see what would happen. To my surprise it performed according to the changes I made. At that moment I felt I had tapped into a new world.

Over the next month, with the help of some computer books, I became quite good at writing basic programs. I hovered over the shoulders of the students who worked on the terminals, pointing out solutions when they ran into trouble. Not much later, I helped teach the very computer class I had never taken, and the following summer I got my first job as a computer programmer. I was fifteen.

My Own Discovery

I learned two different skills independently of each other, without the stiff structure and sometimes unavailable classroom or instructor. Yet both activities were fun, as was the process of learning.

Are the two skills I learned really different? You might say I have a knack for playing the piano or a knack for programming computers; however, the process for self-learning each of those skills was the same. The resources were available, there was an enticing reward, the results could be evaluated, and the process was fun. This is probably the case more often than you might think. No matter how many classes you take or books you read, there is no substitute for learning by doing.

3 The Ten Points of The Ultimate Lesson

Much like the foundation of a house or the spokes of a wheel, *The Ultimate Lesson* has a basic foundation made up of smaller supportive parts. The ten points that make up the lesson are equally important, and each one helps support the whole. Master the ten points and practice them until they become habit. You should then be able to take on just about anything without being dependent upon someone else to teach you.

1. Find the Incentive

It's difficult, if not impossible, to get what you want if you don't know what you want. Setting a goal for a desired outcome is perhaps the most critical factor in making something happen. It seems, however, that many people pay little attention to this driving benefit and doom themselves to work forever to achieve someone else's goals. Your own positive goals will motivate you to get up in the morning and give you enough incentive to follow through until you accomplish them.

2. Enforce the Belief

Without the belief that whatever we desire is possible, nobody would try anything. Lack of belief can act like an insurmountable barrier between us and our goal. Our current belief that we cannot learn something on our own is supported by years of depending on others to teach us. That is a negative belief which must be unlearned if you intend to accomplish your goals independently.

Likewise, positive beliefs have empowered people to climb mountains, break the sound barrier, travel in space, and achieve things that others thought were impossible. Armed with a positive belief, you will find yourself achieving goals that everyone, perhaps even you yourself, may have once believed were impossible.

3. Follow Your Own Guidance

When you set out to learn something by yourself you are your own leader. There are countless ways to guide yourself in the right direction instead of following others. Goal-setting, which you should have done first, will serve as a guide and help you identify the sources of information you will need in order to follow the right path.

4. Begin with Small Steps

Nothing builds confidence better than success. A large, unfamiliar project can be intimidating and frustrating if taken as a whole. But don't give up before you even get started. Take a "baby step" in the right direction by completing a small part of the challenge. A small success can work wonders, increasing your confidence and allowing you to see the whole project as achievable.

5. Learn From Your Mistakes

A child might accidentally touch a hot stove once, but you can bet he won't do it a second time. One mistake can be more valuable as a learning experience than ten successes. A mistake can be uncomfortable or even painful, so it is critical to decide beforehand if you can deal with the discomfort or pain of potential mistakes which you are bound to make.

Some mistakes are acceptable, while others are not. For example, if you make a mistake while learning to walk, you might fall and bang your knee. Making a mistake while learning to drive a car without a driving instructor can cause an accident, injuring yourself or someone else. If you are attempting something where a mistake could endanger you or others, do not try it. Common sense will tell you what you should and should not attempt.

6. Use Patterns

As you progress you will recognize patterns. They may be methods that can be modified and used repeatedly, like piano chords. With a little in-depth vision you will learn that these patterns can be adapted, changed, transposed, and put to use in learning about other areas of your subject. Patterns are rarely limited to what is obvious.

7. Adapt to the Requirements

As soon you attempt to learn something on your own you will encounter all sorts of unexpected problems and barriers. If you can adapt to changes, then you will grow in new ways, and be able to complete your tasks effectively. You will also learn to expect and deal with the unexpected.

8. Overcome the Obstacles

Many of your obstacles will exist only in your mind, like fear, frustration, and intimidation. Everyone has fears, but you should not let fear slow you down or prevent you from achieving your goals. You will learn to eliminate, reduce, or use your fear to help you proceed.

9. Fill in the Gaps

No learning program is perfect. Whether you teach yourself or learn from somebody else, something is always overlooked or left out. When key information or skills are missing, you'll refer to your goals and find out what else you need to learn.

10. Judge the Results

Throughout your process of learning, you will monitor your goals and achievements. You'll stay on track by making periodic changes or "course corrections." Adjustments are common, and can be made at any stage of the learning process. Although it is the tenth point, judging the results should not be considered the last step.

Overview

We will expand on these ten points in the chapters to come. They are the foundation of your ability to teach yourself anything. As you set your goals and begin to learn you will easily recognize when and how each of the ten points comes into play. If you start to drift, or something impedes your progress, refer to the ten points and use one or more of them to put yourself back on track.

4 Find the Incentive

Goal-Setting

G oal-setting is the first and most important step toward achievement. You'll never get to your destination without knowing where you want to go and how to get there. An architect can't build a house without a plan, and she can't draw up a plan unless she knows what her client wants. Many people fail to set meaningful and challenging goals and then wonder why they don't accomplish anything.

Motivation is a Driving Force

Margaret is an Olympic hopeful who gets up at 4:30 every morning to run five miles, then does five hundred push-ups, chin-ups, and sit-ups, drinks a pitcher of raw eggs, and begins arduous training and high-jump practice. Throughout her twelve-hour days of training, Margaret's body begs her to stop and rest, but her motivation to succeed keeps her going throughout each day over the course of many years in this frequently painful daily ritual. She has her eye on an Olympic gold medal. The thrill of victory! Margaret will do anything to be number one, and avoid the agony of defeat.

Now imagine someone who has a tough time getting up at 8:00. Carl slams down a cup of coffee and a pastry, then drives to work, arriving there just in time to punch the clock at 9:00. He waits for two coffee breaks and a lunch hour, then punches out at 5:00 and goes home. Each night he watches the 6:20 sports report and eats a big dinner. On weekends Carl is an "avid sportsman." He wouldn't miss his weekly walk around the block for exercise, or the afternoon football games with his beer buddies. If he can tune his satellite dish to the right signal, Carl and his pals can watch Margaret receive her gold medal and chant, "We are number one."

Both of these extremes are examples of goals at work. Margaret knows the commitment she must make to reach her goal. She knows everyone else wants to be number one as badly as she does, so she drives herself to work hard. She equates her sore and tired muscles with growth. Carl, on the other hand, works for his weekly paycheck and sets aside spare time for weekend football games. He lives for the pleasure of the moment and strives for instant gratification. He'll wait a week for the paycheck (though he probably won't save much of it) and the football games, but any patience beyond that is pushing it.

Carl and Margaret are both motivated by their goals. If she did not believe the gold medal was within her reach, Margaret would never make the sacrifices necessary to achieve it. If Carl didn't need his weekly paycheck to pay for the beer and satellite dish (among other things), he'd probably never get out of bed.

Some People Are Not Motivated

Some people say their mid-life crisis began when they realized that they had spent many years of their lives doing little or nothing meaningful. This crisis is often accompanied by the horrifying realization that the person has no idea what they really want to do. After many years of working to achieve someone else's goals, they try to make up for lost time by spending money and time "soul-searching." If they're lucky they'll break through and find their own worthwhile goals and desires.

We eat when we're hungry and sleep when we're tired, motivated by our instincts just like animals in the jungle. But much of what we're taught as we're growing up turns us away from finding and following our own goals. We're told that if we go to the right school, we'll get a good job. Unfortunately, when it's time to decide which school to attend, we may not have the slightest idea what we'd enjoy doing. Furthermore, a good job that pays well might not provide much enjoyment, while an enjoyable career might not offer an acceptable salary. For example, we assume that all attorneys make a significant amount of money, but not all of them do. When I was working as a legal assistant I learned that many attorneys dislike their work, and the money they earned didn't make up for the lack of enjoyment. While they may have achieved some of their goals, they later found that those "goals" did not satisfy them as much as they had anticipated.

Angela decided to go to law school because she wanted money, prestige, and a "guaranteed good job," not because she loved to study law. Law school was a grind, a day-in and day-out ritual of study, unforgiving professors (many of whom had never practiced law), and difficult tests. Upon graduation, Angela got a job at a law firm. Senior law partners expected significant results from Angela, but gave her the most tiresome work to do. She spent endless hours doing tedious research in a law library and became disillusioned with the glamour of practicing law. If she had loved the law she might have been happy having achieved her goal. But she hadn't thought about whether it would make her truly happy. Her goals of money and prestige had no direct connection to the actual process of learning and practicing law. If Angela had enjoyed the process itself, she would have flourished under the pressure instead of being miserable.

Adequate pay from enjoyable work is possible. Many people are lucky in this regard, but a great number of us fall into the trap of never actively seeking a job we really want. We unknowingly tie ourselves down by creating false limits. You won't know what you can achieve until you open your mind to the possibilities.

Choosing the Right Goals

Whatever you choose to teach yourself, whether your subject is learning a foreign language or starting your own business, choose something you like to do. A fun process is infinitely better than one you can't stand, even if the potential reward is great.

There are two significant parts of any goal: the procedure through which a goal is achieved, and the reward for achieving the goal.

Most of us tend to consider the reward first and the work second. For Margaret, the Olympic athlete, the gold medal (the reward) is a powerful motivating factor, but if she doesn't enjoy any of the training (the work), she probably won't make it to the Olympics. Greater rewards are usually the result of greater effort. Margaret won't win a medal if she doesn't train, and a business won't be successful if the owner doesn't put in long hours and take considerable risks. It's difficult to teach yourself something unless you have a good reason to invest the effort required to learn. Your reason is your reward.

If the reward is enticing enough, you might be able to overlook much of the unpleasant work and just plow through blindly while concentrating mainly on the reward. If you were offered ten million dollars to walk a tightrope strung between the World Trade Center towers in New York, you might drop what you're doing and learn everything there is to know about tightrope walking. You'd probably do it for the reward even though you never had the desire to walk a tightrope. You might even dare to overcome your lifelong fear of heights for such a hefty sum. On the other hand, French tightrope walker Philippe Petit, who actually made that walk, would have taken that, or nearly any tightrope challenge, just for the sheer love of doing it. A reward will rarely be enticing enough to motivate you through a process that you just can't stand, but you'll seldom achieve anything significant where there is little or no reward even if you do enjoy the process.

An ideal goal is balanced between enjoyment and reward. I have always believed that we all have at least one thing that we love to do and that we naturally do well. It just takes a little effort to bring it out. An appealing, enjoyable process might only be missing a proper reward. Be a little creative to find a reward that can motivate you through a project you enjoy. If a basketweaver loves to weave baskets but has yet to find a market for the finished product, an advertisement in the local newspaper could bring in customers. Such an endeavor could launch a business as well as honor the weaver's creativity. Both goals are worthy and motivational.

Even if you like what you're doing, you'll always find that parts of the process are not fun. There's no rule that you must love every minute of it, but that reward at the end will help you get through the rough times and can make the difference between completion and failure.

Recognizing the Wrong Goals

Thinking only of the results or the reward and trying to ignore the process will hinder you as well. A goal approached in this manner will be very difficult to achieve even if it is important to you. A strange thing happens when you don't get enough enjoyment from the process; the hope of a major reward may not be enough to help you overcome the negative feelings you get the moment you sit down to start your project. For example, at one time or another almost everyone says, "I should write a book," but few have the dedication to actually do it. If you do not particularly enjoy writing you might sit for hours looking at a blank piece of paper, sharpening pencils, playing computer games, or changing the ribbon on your typewriter. You would do anything to get out of writing. Suddenly the big reward that loomed so large at the cocktail party when you told your friends you were going to write a book seems less important. You might hear yourself saying, "I'll do it tomorrow." Translation: "Maybe that reward will be more important tomorrow." Guess what happens tomorrow?

Sometimes the process itself really frustrates you. If this is the case, ask yourself if the reward is worth the work. You may decide that the reward or the result isn't what you really want after all. Don't ignore your feelings. Many people consider changing their goals when they come to the painful realization that they're not doing what they want to do. There's nothing wrong with changing goals, but it's better to find out sooner rather than later. Before you commit to a particular goal, focus on the process as well as the reward. If your expectations are realistic, your chances of setting an appropriate, enjoyable goal are good.

33

Doing Rather Than "Being"

Everyone wants to be rich, but few people follow it up by asking themselves what they can do to become wealthy. If someone says, "I have a great idea and I am willing to do whatever it takes to see it through and make it a reality," they're talking about action.

Wealth is the result of achieving a goal, not a goal in itself. Thousands of actors arrive in Los Angeles every week to "make it in the movie business." For each of these hopefuls arriving, there is someone else leaving in despair and defeat. Many of these people desire to be actors so they can have fame, fortune, respect, or perhaps happiness. They watch *Entertainment Tonight* on TV, and when they see the movie stars going to the parties and premieres, they say, "That's the life for me." They might spend money on acting classes that motivate them to keep studying because there's "always a chance." Imagine—a "chance" that you might one day get to do what you have spent so much time training for. Unfortunately, some of these "actors" don't enjoy acting very much. They'd love to be an actor for the high salary, big mansions, and fast cars. If they just didn't have to act, it would be perfect. On the other hand, true actors love the acting process itself and will work on the largest production or in the smallest theater just because they enjoy it. "Being" an actor is merely the result of achieving the goal of acting.

What's worse, many people are actively looking for something that will make them rich quickly so they won't have to work anymore. Is their real goal to be rich, or just to not work? If the only goal is to not work, chances are they'll not be rich. In jobs and even careers people sometimes fall into believing they will "Do this for a while until something better comes along." Doing something now so that you won't have to do something else later will rarely motivate you in a positive direction. It will almost always result in frustration.

Identify the Payoff

When we set out to learn or achieve something, there's always a payoff or reward of some kind, no matter how large or small. This is the part that makes achieving your goal fun. It may seem almost nonexistent, or loom larger than life itself. At Sea World in San Diego, California, Shamu the killer whale and his friends perform two shows a day. They look like they're having fun. The trainers who perform in the show "talk" to the mammals, and Shamu and his friends respond as if they understand and are emotionally involved. The mammals do various tricks to the audience's delight, and right after each trick they are rewarded with half a bucket of fish. They have a clear incentive to perform and they know that if they perform as they've been trained they'll be rewarded.

Clear vs. Unclear Payoffs

A bucket of fish is a clear payoff. Millions of people perform their jobs as they've been trained to do without having much fun, as long as they get their "bucket of fish," also known as a weekly paycheck. They may not dislike their jobs, but their goals have been set by others. Their reward is something tangible, a paycheck, because it would be difficult to motivate them to work for someone else's intangible reward.

Tangible rewards are easy to see but they're not always wholly satisfying. Getting a paycheck, a financial gain from business, or a promotion, are all examples of tangible rewards. Often they come at or near the end of an undertaking and they're strong motivators. For an actor, landing a major part in a movie might be a tangible reward (as well as a primary motivator), and our Olympic athlete Margaret would perceive the gold medal and possible commercial endorsements as her rewards. Tangible rewards by themselves are rarely enough to pull you through a long and difficult process if they're too far in the future. Jane may have to wait a long time before she starts to make the big money that was one of her prime reasons for starting her own business. Margaret couldn't endure years of training merely in the hopes of one day wearing a piece of metal attached to a red, white, and blue ribbon. Everyone needs a little support, encouragement, and fun along the way.

Intangible rewards are usually associated with personal satisfaction. They can also help you achieve interim goals along the way. Jane may celebrate when the first finished product rolls off the production line, even though she is still far from her primary goal of turning a profit. She now feels gratified because she has completed a significant step toward achieving her primary goal. Margaret might successfully perform a difficult routine within a predetermined time, celebrate briefly, and then continue her efforts to improve. Tangible rewards aren't always easy to recognize but they can be valuable when used for motivation.

An ideal motivating goal consists of both tangible and intangible rewards. Let's say your primary goal is to run a business that will make a decent living for you and your family and also allow you to be your own boss. The tangible reward may be "financial independence" or a certain level of monthly income. Some of the interim goals may be deciding what to sell, procuring stock, finding financing, renting a storefront, and the first sale. In many cases the rewards are both tangible and intangible. For example, the first sale is an emotional milestone (intangible) as well as a source of income (tangible).

Accomplishing interim goals will motivate you and give you a little relief from continuously watching and waiting for a reward that is always somewhere in the future. It is natural for interim goals to become part of any significant undertaking, as they help you realize that you are "winning the game."

Long-Term vs. Short-Term Payoffs

Success is directly related to a person's perspective of time. Most successful people are able to think and act with the future in mind, and can handle delayed gratification. A brain surgeon will study for many years before performing surgery for the first time. He can wait until he has finished medical school to earn the income and prestige of a surgeon. This is a clear example of a long-term payoff. On the other hand, a drug user is thinking only as far as his next fix and has virtually no long-term perspective at all. Aside from his next fix, nothing matters to him. He is cursed by his need for instant gratification.

Most people fall somewhere between these two extremes. Is someone who works for a weekly paycheck guilty of needing instant gratification? He is if the need for that weekly paycheck prevents him from doing something he would rather do. In any meaningful activity long periods of time and labor must be endured before gratification is received. Unfortunately, this often goes against human nature. It's no secret that all of us would like to have our rewards instantaneously. Our friends at Sea World aren't going to wait a week or even a day for their bucket of fish. They want it after every trick or they will not see any reason to perform.

At one time or another, every successful person has fought their natural impulse for instant gratification. If you can successfully delay your gratification for the moment and motivate yourself to achieve your interim goals, you will one day reap a much greater reward. If you can set up a long-term goal with numerous short-term goals along the way, you can distribute the gratification over a period of time. This will help keep you motivated as you work toward your reward.

What Does "Realistic" Mean?

Everyone has been told to "be realistic." What does this mean? Who has the authority to judge whether or not someone else's dream is "realistic?" I'll bet that every president of the United States was greeted with this response when they first announced their intentions. You probably heard it when you brought up your latest concept for changing the world. Dream destroyers are a dime a dozen. If you have ambitions that rise the slightest bit above normal it's a good bet that somebody will try to shoot you down before you get started. Those who haven't achieved their own dreams may want to bring you down to their level so they can feel better about themselves. Don't fall for it!

Everyone must define their own reality, and sane folks generally have a reasonable grasp of reality. If you think you're going to fly to Mars next week (or even next year) you're probably not being realistic. However, if you say that you have a brilliant idea for a household product that nobody has invented yet and you aspire to produce it, you might be perfectly realistic. When you voice your innovative ideas, be prepared to ignore those people who say you're crazy. If you run into any of those people, pay no attention. Just move on. They're probably just waiting for their bucket of fish.

Most people's definition of reality stops them from attempting anything meaningful. If this is true for you, your definition of reality should be updated. You can't do so just by telling yourself that you're redefining reality; you must take action. The successful achievement of a short-term goal or interim payoff is a powerful tool in pushing the boundaries of your reality. Identify the real limitations and don't adopt someone else's.

Motivation

Once you've identified the payoff you're halfway there. You know what you're going to "get" after you do the work. Now you have to find the motivation or the "push" to keep you going. There are two kinds of motivation, and both are powerful.

Positive Motivation

Positive motivation is the hope that your efforts will produce a positive result. Running a successful business, playing an instrument, and learning a foreign language are examples of positive motivation and inspiration. It's easy to forget this while you're working if your goals require a considerable amount of effort. Try putting up a sign on your wall or doing something repeatedly to remind yourself of the positive outcome you seek.

While inspiration or positive motivation is useful, it can lack fire. Sometimes you'll have to force yourself to keep going. From time to time you'll catch yourself being lazy. Even though you have identified a clear payoff, you may find yourself procrastinating until you push yourself to get back to work. Don't feel too bad; we're all guilty of procrastination from time to time. But if you allow yourself to get too comfortable, all your goals and payoffs may become less important than your immediate desire (to avoid the discomfort of working at that moment). We like to do what comes naturally and we want immediate comfort. It's unnatural for us to give up that comfort for mental or physical exertion.

Negative Motivation

Negative motivation can be more powerful than positive motivation. You know you shouldn't touch a hot stove, so you would not clean the stove without first checking to see if the burner is hot. This is a reflex action you probably are not conscious of.

It's completely natural to want to avoid negative or painful experiences, but sometimes we can't avoid them. Fortunately, we can use our negative experiences to our benefit. Avoidance can create impressive successes. Some men and women became successful as a result of their unpopularity and low self-esteem. They had a burning desire to avoid failure, and their financial success helped them avoid or suppress their feelings of social inadequacy.

Inspiration is good and can give you incentive to work hard, but desperation can make you work even harder. A balance of inspiration and desperation is most effective. But more often than not, it's the desire to avoid negative experiences that controls most of your actions. Let's say you have a positive goal that requires significant effort. The goal itself may be positive, but the effort required to achieve it is negative. You may subconsciously resist exerting the effort more than you will work to achieve the positive goal. However, if you believe that abandoning the goal will be worse than exerting the effort required to achieve it, you will probably exert that effort. If you must perform one of two negative actions, you will obviously choose the least negative of the two.

Traditional School Motivation

Most of us attend school from our earliest ages through adulthood. Education is necessary, and it does a lot of good, but during our formative years it doesn't teach us much about how to motivate ourselves. Children get more excited about spending their days outside playing than about being in a boring classroom. It's hard for children to understand about future responsibilities such as earning a living and taking care of themselves. The natural tendency is to avoid school (something negative) in favor of having fun (something positive), thereby receiving instant gratification.

School can seem like a job without pay or a contest without a prize. In exchange for sitting in class every weekday, you get a report card graded with the letters A through F, which you have to take home to your parents. If you work hard and get A's, your parents might say, "That's wonderful!" But if you get F's, they're likely to yell at you for several days. If you do just well enough to squeak by with C's, they'll say, "You need to try harder." After you say earnestly, "I will, I will," you go outside and play. Your desire to hear your parents' praise probably isn't strong enough to override your feelings about working hard enough to get an A and having no fun for a whole year.

My elementary school report card system was terrible. It was a vertical graph with class subjects and three grading sections: Excellent, Satisfactory, and Needs Improvement. Four times a year a colored dot was placed in one of the three grading sections. My dots usually stayed somewhere in the Satisfactory section, with one or two of them occasionally creeping into the Excellent or Needs Improvement sections. One day, my fourth grade math teacher, Mrs. Buckley, gave us the option of doing an extra assignment, which meant extra work. She told us that if we completed the assignment we'd get "extra credit" for it. To us fourth graders extra credit meant that our colored dot might move from the Satisfactory into the Excellent section. It wasn't important enough to me to do all that extra work just to move my dot. I couldn't fathom what possible difference it could make, so I opted not to do the assignment. Most of my classmates felt the same way.

When a new and relatively open-minded principal joined our school that year, I learned about motivation. It was the best lesson of my life. Mr. Warner believed strongly in goals and incentives, and tested his theory out at our school. Remember, most grade-school children don't really know what they want to do in life, and they can't be expected to know. In the mid '70s, before the age of home video cameras and VCR's, our school had one of the first primitive videotape systems. It was a bit bulky by today's standards but it fascinated me. I once got into trouble for sneaking out of my class to go watch another class using the video system. I was sent to Mr. Warner's office (a rare experience for me), and was surprised that he did not scold or lecture me as I had feared. Instead, he asked me what I liked to do. I told him how fascinated I was with the video system and how much I loved to play with it. He listened intently, and then told me that I was not in any trouble. I was given permission to go back to my classroom.

About a month later Mr. Warner called my parents and asked them if he could use me to try out his new theory for motivating students. They discussed it with me and I agreed to participate. Mr. Warner set up a point system for me. I received a number of points for doing well in each of my classes. After I received a particular number of points, I was given various small rewards, such as an hour of playing with the video system, but I was allowed to choose one big reward if I earned 300 points. To reach that level I had to do very well in all of my classes, so I knew it was going to be a lot of hard work. Before we started, the principal and some of my teachers met with me to ask me what I wanted for my big reward. I asked for a guided tour of a real TV station, and to my surprise, they agreed.

For the rest of the year I worked like crazy and my academic performance went through the roof. Everyone was amazed at my progress and many people wondered what had gotten into me. My parents were pleased, the principal was happy, and I enjoyed my work much more because I had a reward to drive me. Long before the end of the year I had earned more than 300 points. I marched into Mr. Warner's office with my point cards and a big smile. He praised my efforts, laughed a little, and then he kept his promise. The following week I was given a private tour of a major Boston TV station.

I don't know if they really thought I'd achieve the 300-point level, but I knew I'd do it no matter what. Failing to earn that TV station tour would have devastated me. Mr. Warner was rightfully promoted and left our school the following year, taking his innovative ideas with him. I don't know if he implemented his theories anywhere else, but I'll never forget the lessons that he taught me.

Conclusion

When you choose a goal, look first for what you like to do, then look for a corresponding reward. If the reward means a great deal to you, failing to get it will be unacceptable, and your automatic pilot will switch on to keep you moving in the right direction. Make sure you can clearly identify the reward, whether it's tangible (something you can see or touch) or intangible (feelings, emotions, and the like). Use interim rewards to remind you of your small successes, rather than waiting only for your final big reward.

Once you adopt these principles you'll be able to select and work with worthwhile goals that will keep you interested and motivated throughout your learning process. After you've selected your goal or goals, you're ready to begin learning.

5 Enforce the Belief

Belief and Fear is Learned Behavior

If you believe you can realize your dreams, you are right. If you believe you cannot realize your dreams, you are also right. Once you set a motivating goal you must believe in your ability to achieve it. If you believe you can't achieve your goals, you won't move to make them a reality until you believe that you can.

A belief is probable knowledge, the mental conviction and acceptance of something as true or actual. Our beliefs are so strong, they govern our actions. If you believe in something, you accept it as hard fact and generally do not question its validity. You behave as if your belief was completely real. A single belief can be a powerful tool or a paralyzing hindrance.

A belief is based on the remembrance of an experience. Your memory functions like a quick reference system and can instantly call up your interpretation of your experiences. You probably will not remember the event that helped form a belief, but you remember the result.

A child learns not to touch a hot stove because he has been burned by touching a hot stove once before. Tony remembers the incident well. When his mother said, "Don't touch the stove," he asked, "Why not?" Her answer, "It's hot, you'll get burned," got pushed aside, and his natural curiosity led him to find out for himself. Tony already knew what pain was, from skinned knees and elbows, and other childhood maladies, but that didn't stop him from touching the stove. To him it didn't look like it could do much damage. The blue flame of the gas burner had an inviting quality. Tony touched it, got burned, and screamed and cried for hours.

Tony has learned two things: don't touch the stove, and listen to Mom. He accepted both of these lessons as fact and it'll be a while before he questions them. They're now part of the permanent reference library Tony carries around in his head. Unfortunately for Tony, the beliefs are too broad. He interpreted the experience to mean "never touch the stove," and adopted it universally, when it should have been limited to "never touch the stove when it's on." Tony hasn't touched a stove since, and has never cooked a meal in his life.

Like a belief, a fear is the desire to avoid negative consequences. Fears are formed like beliefs and are similar in function. They can govern your actions much more strongly than beliefs. Take fear of flying, for example. It's common, yet only a small percentage of people who are afraid to fly have ever been involved in an airplane crash. Where did the fear of flying come from, if not from experience? A plane crash is front page negative news which involves death. If someone who is afraid of flying watches that terrifying TV news story about the latest airline disaster, their references of pain, injury, and death are called up and their fear of flying is reinforced. Some people are so scared they cannot even board an airplane; instead they drive to their destination no matter how far. Fewer people are afraid of driving, even though many more people are injured or killed in car accidents than in airplane accidents. There is nothing wrong with a fear of flying, but those who shun the airlines for the open road are operating under the misconception that it is safer to drive than to fly.

Many people are deathly afraid of public speaking. They'd rather have a root canal than speak before an audience or go on live TV. I was a TV news reporter for the Armed Forces Radio and TV Service in the early '80s. During my first couple of years I was quite comfortable doing prerecorded news stories, because I had the luxury of re-recording my voice if I made a mistake. But my first live TV appearance was completely different. Nothing more than a short news brief during a break in the day's programming, I had to read four short news items which had just come over the news wires.

I sat down in front of the camera five minutes before the news brief was to begin. They were the longest five minutes of my life. I started to sweat and my heart was pounding. I thought about the thousands of people who were watching, and right before the "on air" light came on, I felt as if I was going to get sick right there. Twenty seconds after it started, it was over. When I watched the replay, I was surprised at how well the broadcast had actually gone. I didn't look half as bad as I'd felt. I remember the huge difference between how I felt before and how I felt after the newscast, and felt a little silly for being so scared of something so simple. I was afraid of the unknown, which many people will agree is the worst fear of all.

Anytime you try something new, your inexperience or ignorance will be painfully obvious. The unknown elements will rear their ugly heads, and perhaps scare you. Evel Knievel, the famous daredevil of the '60s and '70s, took fear and beliefs to a new level. He was much more than someone who hopped on a motorcycle and jumped over cars and buses. He was a larger-than-life hero who gave his fans an opportunity to vicariously experience feats they wouldn't dare attempt on their own. Knievel theorized that each time he performed a stunt, fifty percent of the people watching were behind him all the way, forty-five percent wanted him to be successful—but if he wasn't they wanted to see it, and five percent wanted to watch him die. Every time he went to work he hoped for the best but, of course, he had no way to predict the outcome.

Most everyone thought Knievel was crazy and had a death wish, but he always said he had a life wish. When he prepared for each stunt he took every precaution and did everything possible to protect himself by making certain the stunt was set up correctly. However, his feats were still extraordinarily dangerous, and each time he put on his red, white, and blue leather jumpsuit he danced with death.

He never disappointed his fans. Whenever he said he would jump, he jumped, and his failures were as spectacular as his successes. If he was afraid of anything, it might have been of losing his personality and reputation. If he'd ever canceled a stunt because he wasn't feeling up to it, he believed his fans would have never looked at him the same way again.

In 1975 he promised to jump over thirteen buses in London. The massive Wembly stadium was completely sold out; more than 70,000 tickets had been snatched up. But when Knievel got over there with his motorcycle and set up his ramps, he discovered that the busses were a little wider than he thought. As a result, his engineers had calculated the jump ten feet too short. His motorcycle was configured to go a speed appropriate for the shorter distance, and he could not travel fast enough to make a longer jump. He called his mechanics in the States and asked them to send a new transmission box that would give him the extra speed he needed.

Show time arrived but the transmission box hadn't. While his advisors were trying to figure out what to do—cancel the show or shorten the jump—Knievel realized that no such decision needed to be made. His fans had paid to see him jump thirteen buses and he wouldn't let them down. He suited up and kick-started his motorcycle, knowing that he wouldn't make it. He gave the performance of his life, suffered the worst crash of his career, and was hospitalized for more than two months. Evel Knievel was more afraid of disappointing his fans than he was of losing his own life.

Fears and beliefs can be powerful motivating forces if they're used effectively. They can be real or imaginary, but more often than not they're taken too far, holding back the believer unnecessarily. As you become more familiar with your beliefs and fears, you'll learn to question them, find their origin, and test their effects. As you test and confront your "demons," you'll gradually discover which ones are real and which are false. Furthermore, you'll learn how to control them and use them for your benefit.

Labels

Labels can be both empowering and limiting. Is a genius smarter than the average person, or is she simply more aware of her resources? I believe that everyone is a potential genius in one way or another. Many of us, suppressed by outside influences, have not tapped into our abilities and resources.

A number of years ago, psychologists experimented with labels and corresponding beliefs of students at an elementary school. With the parents' permission, the students were told that a study had revealed that blue-eyed children were smarter than brown-eyed children. For the next few weeks the students' performance was monitored, with predictable results. The blue-eyed students' performance increased dramatically and the brown-eyed student's performance decreased substantially. Then the teacher told the students that he had made a mistake, and that it was the brown-eyed students who were actually smarter than the blue-eyed students. You can probably guess what happened next. That's right: The brown-eyed students' performance went up and the blue-eyed students' performance went down. A label such as "smart" or "stupid," whether it's given to you by someone else or you adopt it for yourself, can be powerful as a belief or a fear.

Albert Einstein was one of the most brilliant physicists of the 20th century. Imagine what would have happened if he believed he was an idiot. Would he have come up with the revolutionary theories that changed modern physics? Thomas Edison "failed" over 10,000 times in his quest to invent the electric light bulb, but it didn't stop him from trying. If Edison had believed he was a failure it's certain that someone else who thought better of themselves would have successfully invented the light bulb.

Creative people who display an aptitude for art or music are usually referred to as left-brain-oriented. These folks might be writers, artists, or musicians. Logical thinkers and businesslike minds are usually referred to as right-brain-oriented. They may work as accountants or attorneys. The popular notion is that you can only be either left- or right-brained, but never both. This is completely ridiculous. Yet people everywhere buy into this limiting theory. This useless label can prevent an accountant from believing he can learn a musical instrument, or prevent a writer from turning his creative pastime into a profit-oriented business.

I once knew an attorney who had practiced law for twenty years. His parents were attorneys, and their parents were attorneys before them. Though he longed to be an artist, his parents ignored his desire and pushed him to attend law school. They praised his legal achievements and quickly dismissed any mention of art as a passing fancy. They "labeled" him a lawyer (a right-brained or logical activity), not an artist (a left-brained or creative activity). He graduated near the top of his class and was aggressively recruited by the top law firms. After twenty unhappy years of being a lawyer, he realized that he had an unmistakable, undeniable passion for art. He took a chance, quit his job, and devoted his full energy to art. Though he didn't become a superstar artist, he was successful on a small scale and was much happier.

To test your own right- and left-brain skills, try this experiment. Choose something that you'd like to do (it must be something you like) from the "opposite side" of your brain. If you're a bank teller but you always wished you could play the French horn, try that. If you are a freelance writer, try following the stock market. Do one small thing that gives you some enjoyment. Play one or two notes on the French horn or buy a share of stock. Allow yourself an ounce of fun in some other area, and instantly the notion of exclusive left-brain or right-brain orientation will be eliminated.

Learning and Unlearning Beliefs and Fears

Creating Productive Beliefs (and Productive Fears)

A productive belief allows you to take action with a realistic expectation of success. Every achievement, no matter how small, is preceded by the belief that it can be accomplished. If you are hesitant to do or try something new, a belief may be reminding you that you have never been successful in that particular endeavor. If you believed without a doubt that you could do what you wanted, you would jump in with both feet. A well-known motivational question is, "What would you attempt to do if you knew you couldn't fail?"

It's easy to believe that your past experiences are hard facts, but why should a belief relate only to the past? There's little progress in that way of thinking. If you're like most people, you can't predict the future, so you have no way of positively knowing the result until you test your beliefs.

We can make "logical" connections between events that occur repeatedly or simultaneously, but does that make the connections real? Will the wind blow tomorrow just because it blew every day last week? If the wind does blow tomorrow, is it logical to assume it is blowing because it blew before? No, the concept is ludicrous. If you analyze the belief you will arrive at the obvious conclusion that the wind blows because of atmospheric conditions, not because it happened before.

If you set out to do something you have never done before it's as if the wind was not blowing. Don't assume that you won't be able to do it simply because you've never done it before. Configure yourself for success by knowing that you will be successful.

If you have chosen a motivating goal that will keep you going throughout the learning process, you're well on your way to believing it and making it happen. Let's build a belief from the ground up to illustrate this concept. A city skyscraper is a magnificent sight and often a monumental architectural achievement, but it cannot be built in a day. In fact, several years of planning are necessary before actual construction begins. If you wanted to build a skyscraper, and you looked at the project as a whole, you'd probably be intimidated. But if you broke it down into smaller parts, you could manage one part at a time, just like the riddle: "How do you eat an elephant? One bite at a time." After the planning is completed, the first major step is to build the supporting structure and the first floor. A contractor who has built smaller structures may never have taken on a large skyscraper, but he has probably built a single- or two-story building. After the supporting structure and first floor are in place, the contractor repeats what he's done until the remaining floors are in place and the building is completed.

Debbie's goal is to build a new telemarketing business from scratch. She knows she will enjoy the work because she once worked as a telemarketer. And not only did she love the job, she was good at it. However, she's never built a business before. If she tried to tackle the project all at once, she might think, "I'm crazy to even try this!" Just like staring up at the skyscraper, she might become intimidated by the sheer size of the project. Before her neck gets sore from looking up, she'll try to find the "basic structure" and "first floor" of her business idea. No matter how small the first step is, select one you're comfortable with: something you've done before, or something so simple you know you can do it. Your first step is the principal building block in forming your belief that you can achieve your goal. Whenever you hit an obstacle along the way, just take another close look at your own first floor.

Nurture your belief and let it grow. If you can build one floor, you can build two floors. If you can build two floors, you can build three floors, and so on. If you allow your belief enough freedom to expand, your goal will be mentally achieved before you even get started. Make sure the belief grows with useful strength that propels you toward your goal and not with useless obstacles that push you away from it.

Everyone has beliefs that can be used as references. For example, George wants to learn to speak French. He has already taught himself Spanish and believes that French will come easily. I can play the piano, so I also believed that I could learn to play the guitar, which I did. Of course, the two activities need not be as closely related as those.

By the same token, fears can be put to very productive use. If you can create a productive belief, you can also create a productive fear. Bankers and investors are well acquainted with this principle. If you borrow money from a bank to buy a home they'll insist that you come up with a down payment of 10% or more of the purchase price. If the bank is lending 90% of the money, why won't they lend all of it? It would seem as if an extra 10% wouldn't make all that much difference to the bank, but it is a sizable sum to the buyer. The bank wants to be paid on time every month, so the house is collateral that they can foreclose on if you do not pay on time. You would think fear of losing your house would be enough to ensure that you make all the payments, but it isn't enough for the bank. They want you to be deathly afraid of losing your house and your down payment, not to mention the negative impact it would have on your credit report. They have created a fear so powerful that homeowners will do anything to ensure the timeliness of their monthly payments. This fear is productive in keeping homeowners on track.

If you risk something of value to achieve your goal, you've duplicated the bank's "motivational fear" factor. If you're building a business, invest in some equipment. You'll be obligated to create a successful business or you'll lose the outlay. If you're learning a foreign language, plan a trip to that country and buy a plane ticket. If you don't do your homework you won't be able to communicate.

Before takeoff, a jumbo jet accelerates to a point where it's going too fast to stop on what's left of the runway, but it isn't going fast enough to fly. It has gone "past the point of no return," and must continue to accelerate to reach flying speed before running out of concrete. If it doesn't reach flying speed, it'll never leave the ground. It will crash into whatever is just beyond the end of the runway. When you have invested something irretrievable in your goal, you are past the point of no return. You must continue to "accelerate" in order to achieve your goal before you "run out of concrete."

Fear of failure is very common, but few people realize that it can also be a strong motivator. You can put it to good use if you are past the point of no return, but be careful that it doesn't prevent you from taking any action at all when you have not yet started your project. Often this is where most of us end up. Why do we fear failure? Loss, embarrassment, and shattered confidence are the outcomes we associate with failure, and none of these are very pleasant.

Depending on your point of view, failure can be a brick wall that stops you or a stepping stone that gives you a boost. Some of the most successful people in the world have had many more failures than the average person. When these people try and fail, they chose to view the failure as positive. Failure identifies flaws, and instead of stopping the person cold, failure points them in a new direction. To a successful person, "failure" would mean to attempt nothing. These people have put themselves on the line and won't accept anything less than achieving their goals completely.

6 Follow Your Own Guidance

Keep the End Result in Mind

I've worked in large organizations where small groups of people are assigned projects of various levels. Managers of each group are given an assignment, and they work diligently to carry it out by delegating tasks and motivating their people to complete each task. One disastrous day when a boss was getting ready for his vacation, he left an assignment for a manager and her team to complete in his absence. He telephoned the manager and told her the project was on his desk. He asked her to go into his office to get it because he didn't have time to bring it to her before he left for the day. In parting, he said, "Good luck, and I'll talk to you when I return in a month."

The manager retrieved the description of the assignment and set her people to work on it right away. What she didn't see was the CEO's memorandum to her boss, canceling the assignment altogether. The efficient manager saw to it that the assignment was carried out in record time, and she proudly presented the completed project to her boss when he returned from his vacation. When the boss presented the unnecessary project to the CEO, the CEO became enraged and fired the boss.

There was a serious breakdown in communications, but the manager had simply done her job well, and successfully worked her team toward the goal. She guided her group through all of the steps necessary to complete the project, constantly thinking of ways to achieve the objective. She didn't know about the memo canceling the project until after her boss presented it to the CEO. Regardless of the breakdown in communication, the manager was commended by the CEO and given a promotion for doing such a fantastic job.

A leader decides what the project is going to be, and delegates it to a manager, who delegates tasks to his workers, who perform the tasks. In a large organization this arrangement works well and different people hold different jobs. If you work or study independently, you'll be doing all the jobs. You'll be leading yourself, delegating to yourself, and doing the work too. My third-grade teacher once told us that to teach us, he had to know just a little bit more than we did. What did he know that we didn't? He knew how to set and reach goals. If he wanted his students to learn the subject, he had to teach and test them. You'll be acting as your own teacher and student, as well as periodically testing yourself on your subject.

It's critical for you to identify your objective. Break down your goals into bite-sized, identifiable parts, and make sure each one is properly attended to. Change hats as you go from leader to manager to worker. Jane, the entrepreneur, decided that her main objective was to sell her product and make a profit. She must also decide what smaller projects have to be completed before that result can be achieved. Jane begins with the manufacturing of the product. After the product is manufactured, she must arrange for distribution and promotion. As a leader, she assigns each of these jobs to herself as manager, then she puts on the manager's hat and identifies all the tasks necessary to manufacture the product. She does the same with distribution, promotion, and other tasks required to make and sell her product. She puts on the worker's hat and does each of the tasks that she as manager has delegated to herself as worker. From time to time she'll put on the manager's or leader's hat again to check on the progress. Later Jane may take on employees who handle many of these tasks.

This method works well for any level of a project. If you're teaching yourself to speak a foreign language, you'll delegate assignments to yourself, such as completing Chapters 2 and 3 by next week. Someone learning to play tennis might assign themselves the task of successfully hitting 100 balls in a row, or perfecting their serve. You can identify and delegate each part of any subject to yourself. The main difference between going to a school or a job and teaching yourself is that there is no teacher or boss to identify these parts for you. Nobody other than you will press you to follow through.

Finding Your Starting Point

If you want to go somewhere, you simply make sure that every step takes you in that direction. It makes no sense to start moving if you don't know where you want to end up. Start from where you are right now—not literally where you are standing, but where you are in relation to your goal. If you are going into the manufacturing business, can you imagine your product in detail? What is your product going to be, and how will you manufacture it? If you're learning a sport, have you studied the rules of the game? Clearly, certain steps need to be carried out in order. You obviously can't build the second floor of a building before you build the first floor. The first step may be the hardest one you take, because it reminds you that you have many more steps to complete before you see your desired results.

By asking and answering many questions about where you are and what you have at your disposal, you will know what you should do first. If you identify what you know already, you'll have a better idea of what you need to know to reach your goal. As you ask yourself questions you may be surprised at how much you already know about a particular subject. Someone who builds a successful business has usually read about how other successful businesses were built. A person who wants to be a gourmet cook can probably remember a number of great meals they've had in the past. Ask yourself about your chosen subject and write down what you know. As a good confidence-building exercise, ask yourself where you learned these things.

Because you are both the teacher and the student, you must learn to seek out knowledge on your own from various sources as you go. A traditional teacher will follow a course of instruction for class. Most teachers are quite knowledgeable, and many of them have a passion for their chosen subject. Although it doesn't happen very often, it is possible for someone to teach a course without having prior knowledge of the subject. How hard could it be for a teacher to assign some history homework to a class and then give the class a prepared test the next day? When teachers grade tests, they have the answers in front of them. In third grade we were issued a new textbook for a social studies class which had many questions that we used for discussion. Somehow I was accidentally issued the teacher's edition of this book. Right next to each question was the answer printed in red. For about a week I was the smartest kid in class.

One of the most important points of *The Ultimate Lesson* is that you can be your own teacher even if you're not knowledgeable in a subject you wish to learn. You'll change hats hundreds or even thousands of times, back and forth from teacher to student. As the teacher, you'll decide what you must learn because you'll know what you want to achieve. As the student, you'll learn what you've assigned to yourself. Later, you'll go back to being the teacher again to see how well you learned, and decide what should be assigned next. If you did well, you'll decide to move on, and learn more. If you didn't do well, you may demand that you "stay after school."

Supporting Materials

Put on your teacher's hat and decide what materials you'll need to learn your subject. These aren't just knowledge-based materials such as textbooks; they can be any equipment relating to your subject, such as a tennis racket. A huge range of material is available on any subject if you look hard enough. Get your hands on that "teacher's edition" of the textbook.

Books and Tapes

Books are the most common form of supporting material. They range from how-to books to the biographies of famous people who have been successful in life or business. Here we'll divide the books into two categories: study guides and non-study guides.

Study guides can be simple how-to books such as *How to Build a Kitchen Cabinet* or *How to Play Chess in 30 Minutes*, or even *How to Fly an Airplane*. There are how-to books on every foreign language in the world, too. As the computer industry grew, so did the computer book industry. In almost any bookstore you'll find a shelf devoted entirely to books on computers. You can find how-to books on nearly any topic if you look hard enough. These can be valuable tools, but they won't be complete.

Instead, you should use them as just one of many tools in your learning process. Many how-to books recommend additional reading or study materials.

All other books are non-study guides, including general nonfiction books that aren't specifically organized into step-by-step learning guides. They're often invaluable sources of information, and should be used as a supplement to most how-to books. For example, a book on how to be a carpenter may tell you everything about building materials, tools, and how to do the work, but it may not provide any information on how to find clientele. A book on sales might be a good supplement in this case.

If you wish to master a complicated subject, many different study guides and non-study guides are going to be required. You should first identify what you'll need to learn and then prioritize it to determine how to proceed. The best way to do this is to focus on your goal and then work backwards to see what you need to know to reach your objective. If your objective is to build a thirty-five-story building you must first get financing for the project. Then you'll need to know how to build the first thirty-four floors. You'll need to find books on architecture, planning and building codes, zoning, carpentry, and business. Some will be how-to books, and some will be general nonfiction. By working backwards from your objective, you will be able to guide yourself toward achieving your goal.

Related Equipment

It's much easier to learn in practice than in theory. Having the equipment to practice what you are trying to learn is just as important as having the information. If you're learning to play the guitar, you'll need a guitar to practice with. If you want to learn about carpentry you'll need a hammer, a level, a tape measure, wood, nails, and other tools. When you read about how to hammer a nail into a piece of wood, you'll be told to place the nail on the surface of the wood and then hit it with the hammer. However, you won't be told how heavily you must swing the hammer to actually drive the nail into the wood. A book might tell you that you need a certain amount of pressure to drive the nail, but your mind can't interpret this into action without actually doing it. After you drive fifty nails, you'll know how hard to swing the hammer.

People who want to be body builders won't lose weight or gain muscle by reading a book. They must exercise or lift weights. By stressing their muscles and then giving them ample time to recover, they condition their muscles to grow and be ready for ever-increasing challenges. If we see a very muscular man, we assume that he is a body builder. On the other hand, we sometimes think "smart" people are just born that way. The truth is that people who challenge their mind on a regular basis will build up their mental abilities. Using mental "weight-lifting" equipment, you'll be able to challenge your mind just as a weightlifter would exercise muscles in his body.

Using Your Favorite Tools

I once had a history teacher who gave us a strange set of tests. They weren't history tests. Designed to measure how well we learned under different teaching methods, the tests resulted in several different scores with names like Theoretical Visual Quotient and Theoretical Aural Linguistics. The tests supposedly gauged our ability to learn math or language arts by reading or listening. I can't remember what my score indicated, but I know I remember what I hear better than what I see. In grade school I memorized multiplication tables by recording them onto a tape recorder and then playing them back repeatedly. I remember them to this day.

We think in pictures and sounds, and some of us find it easier to remember things this way. To remember the word "boat," think of a picture of a boat rather than just the word "boat." When choosing a personal identification number for a bank card, people tend to pick a combination of letters and numbers that they have already memorized for one reason or another. It could be their spouse's name spelled backwards or their anniversary date, or an easily remembered set of arbitrary numbers. I use a combination of six letters that mean nothing to me. For some reason, I remember the sound of the combination like some people remember a rhyme. It's not written down anywhere, but I can't seem to forget it.

You will find some learning methods are easier for you than others, and perhaps more enjoyable, too. If you enjoy reading, try using books to obtain most of your supporting knowledge. If you are a listener, try books on tape, or record yourself reading the parts of a book that you want to remember. Some people have a difficult time remembering spoken or written words, but they are able to remember every word to a song that they like.

Audiovisual materials are a growing part of learning and can be very useful to you as you go through the learning process. I recommend that everyone become familiar with computers. Computers are one of the best all-around learning tools, and they allow you to tap into many other sources of information. Computers are used so often now, it's becoming harder and harder to avoid them. The educational software market is in its infancy, but soon educational software will be available on just about any subject. Better yet, you will be able to order it right from your home computer.

If you have trouble learning your subject, don't dismiss it as being too difficult. If you come up against a challenge you just don't understand, change the way you learn about it. If it's from a book, record it on a cassette tape and listen to it. After you hear it a few times you might understand it better. Likewise, if you're listening to something and it just doesn't seem to click, write it down as you listen, then read what you've written. Doing this a few times will put the material in a different perspective. It may also help you identify your favorite learning methods. Some learning barriers are not even associated with the subject itself. As you learn, decide what methods and tools work best for you so you'll know what methods to use next time.

Staying On Course

A climber looking at a magnificent mountain on the horizon might say "I want to climb that mountain." Having visualized the goal, the climber packs the necessary equipment—ropes, boots, warm clothing, etc.—and sets out to accomplish it. If she's never been on the mountain, she'll have only a vague idea of the approach she'll take and the obstacles she'll face on the way up, but she'll have a very clear picture of her goal. Even if she knows nothing about the mountain, she knows that the first step toward reaching the summit is to start walking in its general direction. She may stop to talk to a few people along the way and pick up a few tips on what to expect. As she observes the mountain while walking toward it, she may have to adjust her course or change direction slightly to keep the mountain directly ahead. When she reaches the foothills and starts climbing, she'll have to surmount various obstacles on the way up. However, as long as she takes appropriate action to keep moving toward the top, she'll eventually get there.

Whatever your goal, envision it as a mountain on the horizon and then start walking. As long as you keep it in your sight you'll know if you're moving toward it or away from it. You may not know what obstacles lie before you; most difficulties will arise only after you're well under way, and many will not appear until you have progressed beyond the point of no return. Once you are on the way, you'll find that your focus provides you with a powerful incentive to move straight through any obstacles without looking back.

Make Corrections

More concerned with the flight's departure and prompt arrival, a passenger on an airliner may give little thought to the course the pilot follows. He might glance out the window, eat lunch, read a magazine, or enjoy a movie he missed when it played in a theater where he lives. Let's say he's flying from New York to Los Angeles. It might surprise him to learn that the airliner is off course nearly ninety percent of the time. It might make him wonder how any plane ever reached its destination. Were the pilot merely to take off, aim the plane in the general direction of Los Angeles and just let it go, by the time the plane reached the West Coast it could easily be 500 to 1,000 miles north or south of its destination. Variables like weather, the terrain, and the pilot's skill in aiming the airliner at a distant target will have a bearing on the result. What actually occurs is that after the pilot takes off, she takes note of reference points that tell her when she has drifted off course. These references also indicate what the pilot must do to get back on course. Though the plane is headed in the general direction of its destination, the pilot makes hundreds of small course corrections along the way.

Working toward your objective is much like flying an airplane to a distant city. Your destination is clear, so you head off in that general direction. As long as you keep your destination in mind you should be able to recognize when you are drifting off course. Use your destination as a homing beacon. The sooner you spot problems and make the appropriate course corrections, the better off you will be. You may be drifting off course too slightly to notice at first, but if you are off course you will eventually become aware of it. The more off course you are before you spot the problem, the more drastic your course correction must be.

Give yourself regular evaluations. Compare the results of your work to your objective and check your progress. If you don't evaluate your progress, you'll be flying blind, and you could miss your destination by miles.

Don't Complete the Wrong Course

When you're the boss of your own company, you have to decide what to accomplish. If you've ever worked very hard for someone else's benefit, you might have expected something in return such as a promotion or a raise. If you didn't get it, you might have been resentful. What's worse is someone who sets off down a path only to find out that the end result isn't what they really wanted after all. Remember the manager who completed the project that her company was no longer interested in?

When you set a distant goal you may not know if you'll like the result until you finally achieve it. Obviously there was something that attracted you to the idea, so your chances of enjoying the result are good. But be careful of glamour and glitz. When the Indiana Jones movies came out there was a sudden jump in the number of archeology students. Actor Harrison Ford transformed the image of an archeological career into a swashbuckling adventure. I don't think that those who suddenly began taking these classes actually believed they would be wielding whips, dodging snakes, and trying to outrun giant boulders. They may have believed, however, that they'd be involved in an exciting career. Undoubtedly some of them became disillusioned when they began attending courses and found out what an archeologist really does.

As you move toward your goal you'll participate in activities that will give you an idea of what you can expect when you get there. If you enjoy yourself, you may be on the right track. If you don't, then there's a good chance that your goal won't be as fulfilling as you might have hoped. It's a good idea to periodically re-evaluate your goals based on what you've learned. With the new information, you may find that you want to drastically change your goals. If our airline pilot hears over the radio that there is a serious problem at her destination she will select an alternate (and more desirable) destination. During your regular evaluation of your goals, try to eliminate those aspirations that no longer interest you. There's no greater waste of time than working to achieve a goal that is no longer important.

Watch the Winners

Every successful individual or organization has a coach or a mentor. A mentor is a trusted counselor or teacher you can rely upon for guidance and examples. It doesn't always have to be someone you know. Thanks to the media it's easy to follow the successful exploits of most top business people, entertainers, and others of note. A mentor can even be someone who is no longer alive. For instance, a large number of business people are followers of an ancient Chinese warrior named Sun Tzu. His combat tactics, known as *The Art of War* in their many translations, have been adapted for today's competitive business world even though Sun Tzu lived over two thousand years ago.

Finding Mentors

Assuming you are not planning a trip to Mars, chances are good that what you're learning or doing has already been learned or accomplished by someone else. If you're lucky enough to know someone who is knowledgeable in your subject, ask them if they'd like to be your mentor. Ask if you can pick their brain. Many of them will be flattered and offer advice and assistance. Some may offer you a job. However, a few may slam the door in your face, fearing that you'll become a competitor. I'd take that as a sign of encouragement.

You can also follow a mentor that you don't know. You may have some access to this person if, for example, they are a senior executive in the company where you work. If you do, you may be able to get to know them a little. If your mentor is famous, someone you read about or see only through the media, you'll have to follow them from a distance.

Whether you know your mentor or not, do some research. Find out how they started, how they got to where they are today, and what they do that's different from others of similar status. If you know them, ask these questions directly. If you don't know them and they're famous, their biography or interviews may be available in books and magazine articles. Learn about their greatest accomplishments and adapt them to your situation. Find out where and how they learned to do what they've done best. As you follow your mentor you should come away with new ideas and new sources of information. The best question to ask your mentor would be, "Who is your mentor?"

The person you follow need not be in the same field as you. If you want to build your own clothing business you can still learn a great deal by watching an executive who runs an office supply company. Although it's a different field, both must sell products at a profit. If you want to learn French, you might talk to someone who has learned Spanish. If you are planning to open your own retail store, you could take a job in an existing store to learn how it works from the inside out.

There are many different examples to follow. Your subject may be detailed enough that you can learn from several different mentors, each of whom can teach you about your subject's various parts. Continuously seeking out mentors, in or out of your field, whether you know them or not, is one of the greatest benefits available to you. The best part is, it's usually free.

A mentor can be a valuable guide and a good source of information, but don't take everything a mentor says or does as if it's written in stone. Some things will work for you and others will not. Also, be aware that a mentor may have become successful by doing something a certain way which may no longer be practical.

Constantly keep your goal in mind. This will help you to recognize what works and what doesn't work, what is necessary and what is unnecessary, when to listen and when not to listen. It will also guide you in selecting one or more appropriate and inspiring mentors.

7 Begin With Small Steps

We Learn By Doing

The best way to make rapid progress is to jump in with both feet and get yourself deeply involved in your subject. Once you've jumped in it will not make sense to stop, and you'll force yourself to make significant gains quickly.

When you learned to ride a bicycle you may have started with training wheels to learn the basics of pedaling and turning before learning how to balance on two wheels. Your father probably told you how to balance and steer, and advised you to lean into the turns so you wouldn't fall over. You listened to what he said but it didn't sink in until he removed the training wheels. He ran along behind you, holding on until he thought you had the hang of it. Undoubtedly, the first few times he let go you didn't get more than fifty feet before falling.

Your father can tell you a little about what to expect when you ride on two wheels for the first time, but you won't really know what he means until you actually ride a bicycle. When you first try to make a turn, you may not lean into it enough and you may fall over. Remembering that you fell to the outside before, you may lean too much and fall the other way on your next attempt. After about ten or fifteen more falls, you start to get the feel for the right way to turn. You couldn't learn this by just listening to your father without trying it for yourself.

What We Actually Learn

When you learn by doing, your mind absorbs an infinite number of things at once. In bicycling, the theory of balancing on two wheels can be explained and absorbed in principle, but when you ride the bicycle you learn how to coordinate hundreds of muscle movements based on what you see and feel combined with your memory of what you were told. With each trial and error, you subconsciously add the new information to your memory, and use the combination to ride the bicycle successfully.

If you're learning how to play a musical instrument such as the piano, you also unconsciously learn how to move your arm and hand muscles. There are over a hundred different muscle movements in your fingers, hands, and arms that must all be coordinated at the same time. Your brain stores a series of movements that can be recalled as a group, much like a computer program. When you play a song and a chord is required, your brain simply runs the "program" for that chord and your hands and fingers move automatically.

As you learn, analyze your experience and be conscious of what you're learning. It may be much more extensive than it first appears. If a weightlifter strengthens the muscles in his arms he can lift heavier weights, but he is not limited to lifting just weights. He can also lift furniture or heavy boxes. As you learn you are strengthening your ability to teach yourself, and each time you take on a new subject the process of self-learning will get easier.

Repetition Will Make Your Task Feel Natural

If you've driven a car, you're familiar with the gas pedal and the brake pedal, and you can differentiate them by memory and feel. Once you've driven for a few weeks, it becomes second nature. Imagine what would happen if you'd been driving for many years and suddenly the car manufacturers switched the position of the gas and brake. There would be carnage on the streets until everyone unlearned a habit that had been reinforced for years. You'd have to really think about it each time you wanted to go or stop, just to break the old habit and learn the new one.

The way a standard typewriter keyboard is arranged doesn't make much sense to the average person. However, it is widely accepted and almost everyone who learns typing uses that particular key arrangement. If the order of keys were shuffled, experienced typists would start having trouble. They'd have to unlearn the old arrangement and learn the new one.

Our minds have a remarkable ability to perform complicated tasks quickly, but we must first understand what we are doing. As you learn intricate muscle movements in pursuits like typing or playing a musical instrument, slow each movement down until you can consciously understand and digest it. Slow down to a standstill if you must. After you understand what you're doing, gradually increase your speed. It will eventually begin to feel like second nature. You'll be amazed at how fast and efficiently you can perform tasks that once seemed impossible. If you feel a little discomfort, it is probably a sign that you're pushing yourself just hard enough to make progress. Be careful not to put so much pressure on yourself that you give up in frustration. This method works well, and can be adapted for any subject.

Build Confidence: Take Your First Small Step

Your first step toward learning something can be the hardest part or the easiest. No matter how small, it takes you toward your goal and can also be a great confidence-builder. You may feel like a totally different and better person after you take that first step.

Your first step should be as large as your comfort level will allow. It can be a giant leap or a tiny hop, so long as it moves you toward your goal and you're comfortable with the size of the step. Make the first step big enough so that you feel you're pushing yourself a little, but not so big that it causes you to fail or become discouraged.

You can count almost any effort as a first step, but be reasonable with yourself. You probably wouldn't feel that you accomplished much if you just opened the front door and walked for ten minutes, while thinking about what you were going to do that day. However, getting study materials from the bookstore or library, looking at office space for rent or shopping for some equipment are all acceptable first steps, even though they may seem insignificant.

The best first steps are activities that directly relate to the learning process. If you're learning a language, you can study a complete sentence in that language. Use your supporting study materials to translate the sentence, and you'll probably begin to recognize the words and structure of the language. If you take it slowly enough, making sure that you understand everything, you may feel as if you have broken through a major barrier. This will prove your ability to understand, learn, and eventually master the subject you have chosen.

A piano student may choose to start with a simple song that he knows how to sing, such as "Three Blind Mice." Sitting down at the piano for the first time, he hunts for the first note until he finds it. Memorizing that one, he moves on to the next note until he's learned the whole song. Then he practices the notes in succession until it sounds like a song. He's learned a simple song and will have the confidence to learn more. Starting with "Three Blind Mice" is a good first step for a potential musician, but attempting to learn *Beethoven's Fifth Symphony* is probably not an ideal starting point.

A person who wants to start a business might write a business plan as a first step. She should lay out the whole process from her rough idea to her first sale. If her business is manufacturing a new product, she'll start by creating a prototype. If she intends to sell an existing product at a mark-up, she'll buy a few pieces of the product and get to know it inside out. If her business is service-oriented, she'll find out how much her competitors charge for the same service, and come up with ideas for offering superior service for the same (or a lower) price.

These are just suggestions. The first step should come naturally to you. Just remember that it can be nearly anything, as long as you feel you have made a move toward your goal.

Confidence Exercises

Confidence is the natural consequence of learning on your own, particularly after you take that first step. One small success tells you, in essence, that you can do it. Another good confidence-builder is to take a further step in something that you are already familiar with. If a mountain climber has climbed partway up a mountain, he should try climbing a little farther. A weightlifter might try adding a little more weight to the barbell he's attempting to lift. You should choose something that you know well—perhaps something else you learned on your own—and then push it just a little beyond your comfort level.

When you make progress, try to form the widest possible interpretation of what it means. Don't accept the obvious conclusion that you can only "climb a little higher" or "lift a little more." Instead, tell yourself, "If I can climb a little higher, I can probably lift a little more as well." Use your accomplishment in one area to help you accomplish something else.

Pacing Yourself

Small Steps Lead to Larger Steps

A thousand-mile journey begins with a single step, and as long as you travel in the right direction, each step flows naturally into the next. If your steps are too small, you'll feel as if you're not making progress. But if they're too big, they may feel like too much of a stretch. At one time or another, we have all been pushed to do or learn something confusing, something that leaves us totally lost. It isn't necessarily because we can't comprehend the material; it may be that we're not yet ready to understand it. If you begin reading a book at the third chapter, it probably won't make sense, because the information in the first two chapters is missing.

As you take steps to learn, you'll begin to know not only what steps you should take, but how big those steps should be. As a weightlifter builds his strength, he increases the weight on the bar to continue challenging himself. The weightlifter sets goals for his body, such as lifting 200 pounds fifteen times, followed by a thirty-second break, then fifteen more times and another break, then fifteen more times. If he cannot yet lift 200 pounds he has to work up to that level. He'll start with a little weight and increase the weight each time until he can lift 200 pounds over his head once or twice. Instead of quitting at that point, he keeps lifting until he cannot continue. After the painfully short breaks, he attempts two more sets of lifts in the same way. After a couple of days off to let his muscles recover, he tries again. Each time he gets a little further, and eventually he reaches his goal. It keeps getting easier but he doesn't let it get too easy before moving on to heavier weights.

Like the body builder's muscles, your mental ability increases only if you give it continuous challenges. It's tempting to feel good after you've achieved something once or twice, but, like the weightlifter, people who are destined to master their subject won't stop there. They'll continue to practice as they become more proficient. You should allow your task to become comfortable, but don't let it become too easy before increasing your challenge.

Second Nature

You probably do many things during the day that you do not normally think about. If it was an easy day and someone asked you what you did that day you might say "nothing." Think for a moment about what you actually did. You got up, put your clothes on, ate breakfast, walked, and took several thousand breaths, all without thinking about it. When you walk, you don't have to think about putting one foot in front of the other. But remember how hard it was for baby Jody to learn to walk? Walking may have seemed insurmountable to her, but she wanted to do it so badly she just kept trying. However, by the time she was five years old, she probably didn't think about it anymore. The only time she thinks about walking now is when she's deciding where to go.

When an action becomes second nature to you, congratulate yourself. You've reached the highest level of achievement. When a concert pianist gives a passionate performance that earns a standing ovation, he isn't thinking about what notes to play, he's merely performing what he already mastered. He's thinking of the performance as a whole, not merely about which note comes next. A person who speaks more than one language isn't thinking in one language and translating to another, he's thinking in that foreign language.

When you mastered walking you committed it to memory and it will remain with you for the rest of your life. It was so long ago that now you may have to remind yourself that you have the ability to master anything you desire. Choose a simple part of your subject and master it as well as you can. Repeat it until you don't have to think about it as you do it. Once you have mastered a small portion of your subject you will gain the confidence to take future steps. You may have enough confidence to take bigger steps and push yourself a little harder each time.

8 Learn From Your Mistakes

Trial and Error

Learning by doing is the backbone of *The Ultimate Lesson*, and learning from your mistakes is critical to your success. Pay close attention to this chapter, as it is one of the most important.

Don't Be Afraid to Make Mistakes

Anytime you attempt something new, you won't know the outcome until the end. You'll endure a few failures and enjoy a few triumphs along the way, but if you attempt only what you know you can do, you'll find little opportunity for growth. When you try to do something you've never done and you make a mistake, you'll have to change your methods to get different results.

We tend to learn more from our mistakes than our accomplishments. A mistake has significant impact. For instance, if a child misspells a simple word in front of her third-grade spelling class, she won't soon forget it. The experience is so shocking she doesn't make the same mistake again. The child who touched the hot stove remembers his burned fingers all his life.

A mistake also shows us what we shouldn't do. You will always produce results, whether they are what you intended or not. As we discussed earlier, when Thomas Edison was working on the electric light bulb he made over 10,000 unsuccessful attempts. If he'd perceived those attempts as failures, someone else's name might have gone into the history books. Instead, he saw them as 10,000 ways not to invent the electric light bulb, variables that didn't work.

Edison's problem was the light-producing filament that kept burning out in an unacceptably short period of time. He made careful recalculations based on his notes on the materials, their construction, and the test results. He had thousands of variables available to him, and he kept trying them in different combinations. With each "failure" he successfully eliminated another combination of variables that didn't work. Some of the bulbs burned longer than others, so he tried to identify what worked better and then improved on that. His objective guided him and allowed him to identify his mistakes, which he then took the appropriate steps to correct.

Identifying Mistakes

You won't learn much from a mistake unless you realize you've made one. Some mistakes are obvious, some are not-so-obvious, and some are concealed for a long time. When you make a mistake, it's important that you first understand what went wrong and then figure out how to avoid the same mistake again.

Painfully obvious mistakes are easiest to deal with because they are directly associated with what you're doing at the moment. For example, when you play a musical instrument it's quite clear when you've hit the wrong note. If you're baking a cake and you forget to add eggs, you'll know when you remove the cake from the oven. When you attempt to lift too much weight or take too large a step, you can't do it. A painfully obvious mistake leaves no doubt that something is wrong. You'll know that it's the result of your actions.

Mistakes can also be subtle. Something's wrong, but you don't quite know what it is or what you did to get to that point. Let's say you have directions to a friend's new home, and you're driving there in your car. You're supposed to turn left at the second set of lights and then make a series of turns. If you accidentally turned at the first set of lights and then followed the turning directions, you might not immediately recognize your error. However, after a few turns, everything would seem out of place. You'd have to backtrack to find out where you made the first wrong turn. The farther you proceed without realizing this, the more lost you'll become.

Let's say a young man wants to learn Spanish and take a vacation in Spain. He buys a book that was mistakenly labeled as Spanish when it's really Italian. If he doesn't know anything about Spanish he might study the entire book without realizing that he is studying the wrong language. As soon as he arrives in Spain he knows he has a big problem. He has studied hard, but still can't communicate. At first he might think he just didn't study hard enough, and he might go back to study his "Spanish" book heavily for a few nights in a desperate attempt to establish communication. When someone recognizes the language as Italian and brings it to his attention, he realizes his mistake. Now he can take action to correct it. It's too bad that he didn't identify it earlier.

Continuously evaluate your progress and your goal. Once you realize you've made a mistake, break it down to the smallest detail. Do everything possible to understand the mistake and what you can do to correct it. Then try something different. It doesn't really matter what you do as long as you don't make the same mistake again. A mistake is not a bad thing, it's a valuable tool in your learning process. Use it to your advantage instead of allowing it to take advantage of you.

The Safety Net

A safety net is someone or something that can either prevent you from making a costly mistake or help you recover from such a mistake.

When you make a mistake, you've simply produced an undesirable result. You must deal with the consequences of that result, which can vary from one extreme to another. It is critical that you be aware of how severe a mistake you can safely make without causing harm to yourself or others. If you're walking and you take a bad step, you might fall and skin your knee. If you're walking down a flight of stairs, you might be more seriously injured. If you're a high-wire performer in the circus and there is no safety net below you, the fall could be lethal.

When I was learning to fly an airplane I had a flight instructor who seemed to have nerves of steel. Perhaps his experience as an Air Force fighter pilot helped. Nothing that I or his other flight students did ever scared him. He knew exactly how much of a mistake he could allow me to make without getting us into serious trouble in the air. A big part of learning to fly is learning how to get out of sticky situations should they arise. My instructor let me make mistakes that seemed terrifying to me at the time, but he never jumped in to grab the controls. He always allowed me to make mistakes and then forced me to regain control of the airplane and correct my error. We were always high enough in the air so that he would have time to recover just in case I couldn't. I may have learned more about the value of mistakes when I was learning to fly than at any other time in my life. I also learned the necessity of a safety net.

I also tried skydiving. In this kind of activity you must learn very fast or the consequences can be deadly. Prior to my first jump, I learned about skydiving and all the things I had to do while I was free-falling through the air. I learned where the rip-cord handle is, and when to pull it to open the parachute. However, as soon as I jumped out of the airplane and the 125 mile-per-hour wind hit me in the face for the first time, I got a little disoriented. I had about one minute to learn how to get myself in the proper position without flipping over and then to open my parachute and float safely down to earth. On my first few skydives I jumped out of the plane with two instructors who acted as my safety net. This is an extreme example of self-learning where the motivation to learn (and to survive) is at a maximum, and there is no room for a mistake. It is also an example of a situation for which you need a safety net. I couldn't have done it safely without the two instructors who jumped with me.

In some cases the cost of making a mistake is too great. You can't train yourself to be a surgeon by operating on someone to see what works and what doesn't. You wouldn't practice balancing on a tightrope suspended high in the air where a fall could be fatal. You can't learn how to fly an airplane without having an experienced pilot with you. Obviously, any activity that could result in harm to you or others requires a safety net. A medical student will first watch an experienced surgeon, then she will assist in numerous operations before performing even the simplest surgery by herself. An aspiring tightrope walker would use a net or suspend the tightrope only a few feet off the ground while learning.

While you're learning it's important to think about minimizing risks. If you want to learn about investing in the stock market, start with a small sum of money. You wouldn't put all of your money on the line before you know what you're doing. Losing a few hundred or even a few thousand dollars is a valuable learning experience, but losing all your money would only teach you the stupidity of taking too large a risk. Part of your job as your own teacher is allowing yourself to make mistakes while managing the potential risk. Carefully analyze the risks before you begin. Focus on how to minimize them, ask yourself if you can deal with the consequences of a mistake, and decide if you need a safety net.

Allow trial and error to be your ally in learning, and treat mistakes as learning tools. Don't ignore the potential consequences of your mistakes and, above all, don't put yourself or anyone else in jeopardy.

9 Use Patterns

Recognizing Patterns

As you learn, you will notice patterns. When you can identify a pattern, you can expand on it and use it to learn many different aspects of your subject. There are several kinds of patterns and you'll notice that some of them are quite a bit easier to recognize than others.

Distinct Patterns

The piano keyboard was the first pattern I recognized. As I learned the notes, I experimented with different combinations of them. As I observed their relationships, I could see how far apart they were on the scale and hear how they formed chords. I moved up the scale a half-step and formed an entirely new chord with the same pattern of notes. Later, I moved up another half-step using the same pattern. That's when I realized the pattern worked for the entire piano keyboard. Instead of learning just one chord, I had learned how to form that chord anywhere on the piano simply by transposing the pattern of notes.

Computer programming patterns also worked well for me. Computer language is fairly straightforward, making it easy to experiment with different lines of computer code to get different results. There were both large and small patterns throughout the programs, and by trying them in different ways I made the programs do much more than the textbooks intended.

Languages also have easily recognizable patterns. As soon as you understand basic sentence structure you simply practice with the various nouns and verb conjugations, word definitions, and tenses. The sentence structure won't change. As soon as you understand a pattern, the rest makes sense and you can use the same pattern over and over again.

These are all clear and solid patterns that are fairly easy to recognize. They're also easy to follow and probably won't change very much. Every subject has patterns, and if you can find them, they can be valuable learning tools. They are one of the first things to look for.

Indistinct Patterns

Indistinct patterns are hard to recognize and even harder to follow. One of my favorite indistinct patterns is economic trend-watching, where "experts" predict the activity of the economy or the stock market. They analyze market history, dissect complicated charts and graphs, run sophisticated computer programs, and then "predict" the direction of the stock market or the economy. After the market changes, they take credit for being right, or scramble to prove their erroneous theories. They'll never admit, even to themselves, that they were just plain lucky or unlucky.

The stock market and the economy go up and down at will. Every now and then a news story describes an experiment in which an "expert" stock analyst is pitted against a monkey pointing at random to a stock list. The investments they "select" are bought and held for about a year and the results are analyzed. More often than not the monkey comes out ahead. Furthermore, most investment managers include a statement on their prospectus to mildly warn future clients that "past performance is no guarantee of future results." This is sometimes pointed out to investors after they've lost a substantial amount of money.

Human behavior is also a difficult pattern to follow. It's hard to predict behavior without knowing a great deal about the person in question. If any part of your subject involves interpreting patterns of human behavior, you should attempt to learn what you can about the people you're studying. Find out as much as you can about their beliefs, and what they expect from life. Learn about their motivation, what they want to happen in the future. Belief and motivation are two of the most prominent driving forces in human behavior. A little insight into them can go a long way, particularly in a business situation where you must understand your potential customer's needs.

Transposing a Pattern

The key to utilizing a pattern is being able to transpose it. When a pattern in one area has been transposed, you can use it to guide you through another area.

Get to the Root of the Pattern

You can find recognizable patterns in the simplest of subjects. The key to finding them is aggressive aware-ness. Scrutinize your subject and isolate the smallest de-tails that repeat themselves. In spelling, for example, the letters "ie" make a particular sound and are used fre-quently to form many other words. You'll run into excep-tions such as the spelling rule "i before e except after c." In this case, the exception is part of the pattern.

Picking out combinations of musical notes and lines of computer language is relatively easy because they al-ways produce the same result. After you identify the smallest elements of the pattern, take it to the next level. Group those elements differently and see if they form another pattern of their own. Remember that the pattern will be composed of combinations of the smaller ele-ments that you have already recognized. Study the small elements individually, then put them together to form larger patterns. Do they form patterns of their own?

Start looking for patterns as if through a microscope, and step back now and then to view the larger picture as if you are looking down from an airplane. Some of the larger patterns are quite easy to see, but don't be satisfied until you are sure that you have analyzed the pattern to its smallest elements. It's important that you understand the smallest parts of the pattern before you fully utilize it even if you can clearly see a larger pattern. Once you reach what you believe is the smallest level of the pattern, try to break it down even more. You'll often find an even smaller pattern that you didn't suspect existed.

Adapt the Pattern

After you have recognized a pattern, adapt it to your needs. Move the pattern to a different part of your subject and experiment with it. Though you'll have some idea of where to use the pattern, you may have to fine tune it a little to make it work.

In the spelling example, the letters "ie" are used in many words. In playing piano, the patterns of notes can be moved anywhere on the keyboard to form different chords. A simple sequence of notes or chords can be repeated and adapted to make a song. Many songs consist of a simple repeating pattern of chords or notes with a few variations. Once you've learned a sequence you only need to learn how many times to repeat it to play the whole song. Computer programming works the same way. Small patterns of computer language are bundled into groups that perform routine computing operations. To create a program you'll decide what you want it to do and then arrange the patterns in the sequence that will give you the results you want.

Adapting and transposing patterns work well when you have a solid pattern, but when you're dealing with a vague pattern like human behavior, try to concentrate on motivation and belief. If you own a business and have employees, you'll notice that their performance is strong when they have an equally strong incentive to perform. (Make sure it's more than just a bucket of fish disguised as a weekly paycheck.) If they believe they'll be rewarded for taking initiative, they'll give you more than you ask for. If they fear dire consequences for making even a single mistake, they may not be inclined to try anything creative.

Don't drive yourself crazy looking for a pattern. Most subjects will have patterns that are fairly easy to identify. If you're stuck in a futile effort to find a pattern, stop looking and move on. Recognizing and adapting patterns can be a useful tool, but it may not be relevant to every part of your subject.

10 Adapt to the Requirements

Conditioning Your Mind and Body

If all your life you were trained to let others teach you, you'll most likely need some time to adapt to the self-learning process. This kind of adaptation is nothing more than remodeling your old habits into new ones. With the right kind of motivation it will come naturally.

The Disadvantaged Have an Advantage

Some of the most brilliant musicians are blind, such as Ray Charles and Stevie Wonder. Would they have been as brilliant in the field of music if they had been able to see? It's clear that they didn't have the "distraction" of sight to deter them from concentrating on the sound of the music. Since they rely completely on their ears, their interpretation of sound is much more sensitized. They turned what most people consider an extreme disadvantage into a powerful advantage.

A number of years ago, *60 Minutes* ran a story about a remarkable woman who was born without arms. She did nearly everything a normal person could do. She prepared food for the family, wrote letters, gave her son a haircut, and put on her own clothes, all with her feet. It was normal for her. She'd been practicing all her life, because she had no other appendages to use. She chose to learn to use her toes and feet in place of the missing arms and hands. Otherwise she would have been dependent upon others to do everything for her. If a pair of arms was miraculously attached to her shoulders, it would feel awkward, and it would take her some time to learn how to use them.

Most of us have had two arms and two hands all our lives. They feel normal to us and we haven't had the incentive to learn how to do very much with our toes and feet. If you woke up one day with four arms, you probably wouldn't know what to do with the extra two. Try to imagine going through life with two arms if everyone else had four arms. You might feel a little envious, but you wouldn't feel totally disadvantaged because you would have done everything as you have using just two arms.

For those with disabilities, the motivation to adapt can be powerful. However, there is no reason you have to be desperate or lacking to take advantage of this kind of powerful motivation. During your goal-setting you will have identified many powerful incentives to help you to adapt into an expert self-learner.

The Stress and Recovery Cycle

Athletes know a great deal about the cycle of stress followed by recovery. You're probably familiar with stress, but how much do you know about recovery? If you lift a heavy weight or run a long distance you're putting stress on your body. After such physical exertion, you're probably exhausted. Exhaustion is your body's way of telling you to let it adapt to the stress that's being thrust upon it. Most of the results of physical exercise usually occur during the recovery period. During this inactive time your muscles are growing, adapting, and reorganizing themselves to accept higher amounts of stress. If you continually stress your muscles without allowing them sufficient time to recover, they won't have an opportunity to grow.

Your mind works the same way. If you challenge it on a regular basis, it adapts to the challenges and grows stronger. Like athletic activity, you can feel intellectual improvement as tasks that once seemed challenging gradually become easier. Recovery is just as important for your mind as it is for your body. If your mind is under constant stress without time for recovery, the result will be burnout instead of growth. As you begin to learn on your own, you will slowly adapt and build your mental "muscles," adapting and increasing your natural intellectual ability to learn by yourself.

Allowing Yourself to Adapt

Adaptation and growth can sometimes go unnoticed. They are so gradual at first, much like a plant growing, that if you look at them every day you won't see much progress. If you test your ability after a month or so, you will probably notice significant development. You will suddenly notice that your tasks are getting much easier. After you've seen this a few times, you'll gain a tremendous amount of confidence.

Learning should also be natural and relaxed. You should be able to monitor your progress and see results, so if you're not growing at all, there are a few things you can do to help yourself along.

Take a Different Approach

If you haven't made progress, back up and take another look at what you're doing. Are you moving in the right direction? If your assignment seems overly difficult, it could mean that you missed an important step along the way. If that's the case, retrace your steps until things make sense again. You'll probably find good reasons to backtrack. Retracing your steps is perfectly acceptable. Being thorough is more critical to learning than speed is. The only teacher grading you is yourself.

If your steps feel too large, try taking smaller steps. If you missed something along the way, the steps you are attempting might feel a bit drastic. You may find that you push a little too hard at first. Keep experimenting with ever smaller steps until you feel comfortable. They need not remain small forever; this may be just a temporary regression or correction. Allow the process to flow naturally, you'll know when to increase the pressure again.

If you still have trouble, perhaps you should take different steps altogether. Turn your problem around, look at it from a different angle, ask someone for advice, or just try something else, anything to get yourself going again. Don't be afraid to experiment with something completely different from whatever you did before. Try exploring another part of your subject for a change. You may find yourself enlightened by something that you missed along the way.

Try skipping ahead just for fun. If you give yourself a chance to see a preview of coming attractions, you might feel some new motivation for upcoming material or activities. This goes hand in hand with giving yourself periodic rewards and enjoying the process rather than waiting for a distant end result.

Don't Hold Yourself Back

Adaptation is a natural, and you should be automatically adapting to whatever challenges you give yourself. If you don't feel as though it's working for you, look for signs that you're holding yourself back. If you're not enjoying yourself, you may need to do something fun or take a short break. If you've lost sight of your objective, you may need to take time to refocus your goals. Ask yourself as many questions as possible, try some different activities, and refuse to rest until you have identified the roadblock.

11 Overcome the Obstacles

Intellectual Obstacles

Obstacles are common in just about everything you do in life. Many obstacles are only in your mind, which can mean they are the easiest to handle. At the same time they can also be the toughest.

Fear

False Evidence that Appears Real is a good acronym for fear. It prevents more people from taking action than almost any other obstacle, even though it's only in their mind. There are activities that some people fear and others do not. Fear is dread, anxiousness or apprehension accompanied by a desire to escape pain or evil.

When I was twelve years old, I delivered newspapers on my bicycle in the morning, like many young boys do at some point in their lives. My route was on quiet residential streets. Every day I rode around and dropped off the papers, usually finishing my route by 7:00 in the morning. I only had three problems: dogs. One of them barked and chased me away from the front door. Another chased me all the way down the street. The third dog was the biggest problem of all. I'll never forget the first time I met the giant German shepherd. His house was near the beginning of my route. I rode my bike into the driveway, parked it, and walked up to the front door. Then I saw him staring at me like a wolf ready to attack. Like most twelve-year-olds, I felt my early death would be unjust, so I ran out of the yard and across the street. The dog chased me, but stopped at the end of the driveway where he sat down and waited. Unfortunately, my bike was in the driveway and I was too frightened to retrieve it. I had to run home to get my dad out of bed to come help me. Dad grew up with dogs and had no fear of them at all. He waked in and got my bike with no problem. The dog didn't even approach him. Clearly I could have done the same, but I sure didn't believe it at that moment. I imagine the dog knew that too.

Skydiving was another of my lessons in fear management. I decided to take the skydiving class for the thrill of it, but also because I wanted to confront my fear of the unknown. As I drove up to the "drop zone," I remember wondering if my affairs were in order, just in case I didn't live through the jump. I learned everything I could

110

about what I had to do. I learned about parachute malfunctions and what to do in the event of an emergency. I was confident that I knew enough to make the jump successfully, but an element of danger remained. Nothing can quash the fear of a first-time skydiver standing in the open door of an airplane at 12,500 feet about to step off into who knows what. But as soon as I jumped, it felt like my fear disappeared. There were too many other things to do during that one minute of free-fall. It was life or death and I had no time for fear. I was committed to doing exactly what I had learned on the ground or I would have had trouble. In the end everything went smoothly, and when I landed I wondered why I'd been so scared of something that turned out to be so much fun.

The truth is, when facing a terrifying event, most of our fear occurs right before the event. Many famous performers get terrible stage fright just as the curtain is about to go up. But during the performance, their fear subsides or disappears entirely. After you've experienced this a few times, you'll realize that most of your fear begins and ends in your mind.

Common fears are associated with the unknown. We are creatures of habit. Once we get used to something, changing it is difficult. People who want to be rich or successful sometimes find they really don't want to make the changes necessary to achieve those goals. This leads to the most insidious fear of them all, the fear of success. Fear of success lurks in your subconscious and when you're least suspecting, it sabotages you. You probably don't even know it's been there.

Why would anyone fear getting what they want? Because the fear of trading in that old familiar feeling in return for what's unknown is often greater than the desire to succeed. Much like a heating and air conditioning system, you set your comfort level like a thermostat and regulate it. If you get too uncomfortable, the "heater" or "air conditioner" brings your comfort to the appropriate level. While you'd think success would be comfortable in any form, with it comes many unexpected, disquieting changes. Even if you dream of massive success, you may unconsciously return to your comfort level if things get a little too hot. If it happens to you, turn up your "thermostat" and allow things to move a little faster. Learn to fear that non-productive comfort zone which doesn't take you anywhere.

Achieving goals or mastering a subject requires discipline and persistence. We're naturally impatient, and the idea of suffering pain or discomfort to obtain a future reward is foreign to us. When we decide we want something, we want it now. We don't want to wait and we usually don't want to make any sacrifices.

Eliminating fear is similar to building a belief. Faced with a large task or complicated project, the fear of failure can appear greater than the task itself. Just like a belief, identify a "first floor" or basis of the fear. Find some part of your project that isn't essential to achieving your goal. If you tried it and failed, would it destroy the project or would it just slightly change your plans? Attempt it anyway. You'll probably succeed but if you fail it won't make much difference. If you can do that, you've sliced the fear into smaller and easily digestible pieces. After you destroy one small fear, allow that victory to extend to your other fears. In a sense, you are saying, "If I conquered one thing, I can conquer another."

Fear of failure can be just as devastating as fear of success. As Thomas Edison showed, it's possible to eliminate this kind of fear simply by looking at failure as the result of achievement. From his results, Edison learned to avoid repeating his mistakes. Successful people view failure as advancement. They know that they're driving without a roadmap. They'll inevitably make some wrong turns, but it's better than not going anywhere.

Some fears are more ingrained and require a greater force to push them out. You can take another fear and use it to propel you away from the one you're trying to eliminate. If your fear of failure paralyzes you so much that you can't even begin your project, try focusing instead on the consequences of doing nothing. See yourself several years down the line having never pursued your dreams. Whenever you feel yourself hesitating, replay this depressing result in your mind and feel the pain of having done nothing. Remember that failure can teach you much more than success. If fear prevents you from doing what you want to do, look hard for another fear (create one if you have to) that scares you into action.

Discomfort

It's normal for you to want to feel "natural" at whatever you're doing. When something isn't familiar it's going to feel awkward. If it feels awkward, pat yourself on the back. You're probably growing. It may feel difficult to remember and pronounce words in a foreign language, and it may feel awkward to play a song on the piano at first, but since you're moving in a positive direction, you'll soon adapt. Each time you notice this discomfort be glad, because it's an indication of progress.

If you feel too much discomfort, stop and reevaluate your course. If you're moving in the wrong direction, then your discomfort is a useless waste of energy. For example, if you're a musician and your hands are sore from playing, that's good. If you're a guitarist who plays until his fingertips bleed, that's not good. If you feel stress because the material is a little difficult to understand, that's good. If you're blindly studying with a headache and losing interest in the material, that's not good. Common sense will guide you in knowing when discomfort is productive and when it isn't.

Frustration and Exhaustion

If you reach a point where you feel totally depleted, when you just can't take another step, then congratulate yourself. You've gotten the most out of yourself physically, mentally, or both. A weightlifter is never sure just how much weight he can lift. He won't simply stop after lifting a certain amount of weight just one time. He'll put more weight on the bar or go for more repetitions. He won't be satisfied that he has gotten the maximum from himself until he fails in his attempt to lift the bar. When he reaches this point he takes a shower and goes home feeling fulfilled.

If you feel frustrated when you try to exert that last ounce of effort and just can't do it, you too should feel fulfilled. You've earned a break and a chance to recover. If you continue at this point without a break it will probably be counterproductive. After you have recovered, pick up where you left off. This time push yourself even further. Frustration and exhaustion are accurate indicators of your true potential. If you consistently push yourself to this point you'll go further each time.

Lack of Belief or Negative Belief

Negative beliefs can prevent you from taking action. If you think you can't do something, you probably won't attempt it. One of the most famous limiting beliefs in history was that the world was flat. In the late 15th century there was plenty of "evidence" to support this belief. Nobody dared venture beyond the horizon for fear they'd fall off the edge of the world. Christopher Columbus had a different view. He believed that the world was round, but with no evidence to back up his theory, he had to be courageous and risk his life to find out the truth. Everyone thought he was crazy. Columbus proved them wrong, discovered the New World, and destroyed what may have been one of history's all-time greatest limiting beliefs.

We're all guilty of holding onto limiting beliefs or "the-world-is-flat"isms as they are sometimes called. "I'm just no good at sports." "I don't seem to have the knack for math." "I'm not attractive enough for a date with the prom king or queen." These are all examples of limiting beliefs. If you think you're no good at sports, did you try as many sports as possible and find nothing that you enjoyed? If you have a problem doing math, have you broken down the challenge to find the "first floor?" Did you ask the prom king or queen for a date? Did they answer "No"? If they answered "No, I wouldn't be caught dead with you," are you really interested in going out with such a rude person? By questioning your beliefs from all angles you challenge them and quickly find out if there's any real evidence to back them up.

If a limiting belief sticks with you, dismantle it piece by piece as you would dismantle a limiting fear. Try taking smaller steps to help yourself gain confidence and build up your positive belief in stages. Watch someone else successfully do what you believe (at that moment) you can't do. Never succumb to the notion that your beliefs and fears are carved in stone. They're only temporary roadblocks that can be eliminated with a little conscious effort.

Physical Obstacles

Mental obstacles are not the only block in learning. You'll encounter physical obstacles along the way as well. These can be dealt with almost the same way as mental obstacles. You'll find that some of your perceived physical limitations are merely mental limitations. You can often overcome them simply by looking at the situation in other ways.

Lack of Capital or Equipment

"This is going to require a load of cash! Where are we going to find that much money?" Entrepreneurs around the world complain about the lack of capital every day. If you're attempting to raise money for a business or entrepreneurial venture, you may never raise "enough." Some people raise half a million dollars and fret that it isn't enough to get started. Others start with fifty dollars and build a million-dollar business. If you're not planning to mass produce computer chips or automobiles, you can probably start out on some scale with almost no money at all. Some of the most successful companies in the world started with a home office operated from a kitchen table. If you don't think you have enough money, re-size your capital requirements. If you were planning to start big, think a little smaller. Instead of building a factory to manufacture your product, make a few units in your basement. Get your friends to work for you in return for a share of the potential revenues. Find creative solutions to your financial requirements.

If you're learning a skill that involves a musical instrument or other costly equipment, try to find inexpensive alternatives that you can easily get your hands on. A small electronic piano keyboard or a couple of barbells are within just about everyone's reach. A Steinway grand piano and a full workout machine may be a little too much of a stretch right at the start. They are probably unnecessary as well. Secondhand stores often have slightly used equipment at incredibly low prices.

117

Age

"I'm too old to do this." I'd be willing to bet that this person once claimed that they were too young to do something. Age is a common excuse for shortcomings or negative beliefs. In the corporate world, age and status play a significant role in one's career and advancement, but in the "real world" your actual achievements and abilities are gauged, without regard to your age. Some people started their own business when they were as young as ten years old, and others have climbed mountains at the age of seventy or more.

Time

"I don't have time." This excuse is one of my favorites. If you don't have time to devote to achieving a goal and realizing one of your deepest desires, what do you have time for? Do you have time to sacrifice your life for others to help them achieve their goals and desires?

If you don't already have time management skills, you should develop them. Activities that move you closer to your goals obviously take precedence over activities that keep you away from your goals. Do you have enough time to pursue your goals? Your day job, the phone, and the chores all appear to require your immediate attention. Unfortunately, most people habitually deal with these interruptions at the moment, whether they are important or not. If you can identify and perform important tasks and put off unimportant tasks, you will have mastered the essence of time management.

Ability

When you try something new it may feel strange at first. There will come a time when you feel that you can't do it. You'll think, "I'm just no good at this." Whatever "this" is, as long as it's something you truly enjoy, you have the potential to be good at it. If, after trying something for awhile, you find yourself starting to say you're not good at it, in a sense you've reached that level of exhaustion which means you got the most from yourself. Take a short break, recover, and jump back in. If you physically cannot do something, always check to see if it's just an intellectual block. Remember that every task, whether mental or physical, becomes more comfortable with repetition. Be patient, be persistent, and don't give up. It'll come to you.

12 Fill in the Gaps

Identify What Is Missing

When you're teaching yourself, from time to time you'll find gaps in your knowledge. You won't always know how to proceed, and some things will get left out. It's up to you to identify these gaps and fill them in to become proficient in your subject and achieve your goals.

Find What Works

When I was in Seventh grade, I prematurely ended up a Latin class that I didn't like very much. I didn't understand it, and did poorly in the class, but my teacher thought it was lack of interest causing the problem. Some time later I took a basic English class and only then did I understand why I had so much trouble with Latin. I hadn't learned enough formal English. I knew how to speak and write naturally, but I wasn't well versed enough in sentence structure to comprehend the Latin material. The English classes I had taken before obviously lacked some important basics. The one class I took later filled in the missing elements and the Latin class suddenly began to make sense.

If part of your subject gives you trouble, you may have missed some critical component. Unless you can identify what's missing, you may get frustrated with what you are trying to learn at the moment. Time to backtrack. Keep going back until you hit a point where you understand the material clearly. Then the part that you had trouble with will start to fall into place.

My father was a nuclear physicist. When I was a child, he had a hard time explaining his job in a way that I could understand. He said I'd need to have a background in physics to comprehend what he was talking about. This means we aren't dumb about anything, we just may not have learned all the necessary background yet. You or I could understand nuclear physics if we had the desire to learn it, and invested the time educating ourselves. We'd start at the "first floor."

The Gaps Will Show Themselves

Finding the gaps in your knowledge is very simple but time-consuming. They'll quickly appear as you start backtracking. Make sure that you thoroughly understand the current material you're working on before you move ahead. Occasionally you might discover that you're in a rush to get to the next level. If you're comfortable with it, take the next step, even if it seems a little premature. Be sure to review what you've learned as often as possible to make sure you're not stepping over anything that you'll need later.

If you feel you don't understand something, be as specific as possible. Look for the smallest part that you don't understand rather than accepting the generalization that you don't understand any of it. Ask yourself what part you don't understand. If you do, your answer will help guide you to the gap quickly. Presumably, you will also be faced with a much smaller gap to fill.

If you can't find the gaps, put on your teacher's hat and think about your objective. You can judge your progress by keeping your objective in mind (unlike a traditional classroom, where only the teacher is fully aware of the objective).

Priority and Sequence

You've started learning, and you're having fun doing it. Suddenly you're faced with several tasks that seem equal in importance and you don't know which one you should do first. If it seems like you've missed a step, try to identify the preceding step, even if you didn't complete it. Maybe you missed one key element, or maybe several. If several elements are missing, you'll need to identify them. For instance, the supporting elements of the roof of a house are the four walls. Each of those supporting elements may lack some smaller supporting elements. In my Latin class, the missing element was clearly basic English.

Backtrack in an orderly manner until you find a task that you're able to perform. In this way, you can better understand the next level and support the next task. The priority of the elements or tasks should become clear. If it doesn't, continue going back even if you must go over things you've already done. Maybe some elusive elements at an even lower level are necessary to understand the current level. However, they may not have been necessary during some of the earlier tasks.

Once you recognize priorities, you should be able to guide yourself fairly easily. Stay on top of your agenda, and chances are you'll have little trouble keeping your priorities in order.

13 Judge the Results

The Judgment System

Being your own judge is just as important as being your own teacher. Progress isn't much good if it takes you in the wrong direction. You must develop the ability to know when you're making progress in the right direction and when you must change course.

Knowing What You Desire

The first point of *The Ultimate Lesson* is "Find The Incentive." Looking at a car's speedometer gauge, let's say your goal is to reach a speed of 60 mph. You can clearly see your goal on the speedometer, and as you accelerate, you can watch the little needle climb the scale. You know that you are halfway there when it hits 30 mph so you need to keep accelerating. When the needle finally hits 60 mph, you know you have achieved your goal.

As you move toward your goal, pay close attention to the indicators, much as you would check your speedometer. Some indicators will represent your objective (the 60 mph indication) and others will indicate where you are presently (the little needle that indicates your current speed). If you're building a business your main goal would be to make a profit. Where you are at the moment might indicate that you're about to finish manufacturing your first run of products. Or your current indicator might show you that you've sold half of your inventory and are a measurable distance away from profitability. From this, two things will be clear: your distance from your goal, and whether or not you've moved closer to your goal. This is the basis of your judgment system.

You should use these indicators to judge your progress at all levels. As you learn, you will break down your subject or goal into small units of achievement. If you can set up this judgment system for each task or level that you want to achieve, and if you have properly and effectively set your goals, judging your progress will be easy.

From time to time you may have difficulty judging where you are relative to your goal. Backtracking works well here also. Much as you would identify the gaps that need to be filled in, you can backtrack in your judgment. If you don't have a clue how close you are to achieving your goal, or don't know if you're even moving toward it, take another look at the lower levels. If Jane wants to find out how close she is to completing the manufacture of her product, she must look back in judgment, getting more and more specific, until she reaches the level where she can see that she achieved something measurable.

Continue to watch and study the winners in your field. You'll see their achievements and, with a little research, you can study them in depth. Identify the steps they took to get to where they are today. Watch their progress and just for fun try to guess what their goals were.

Course Corrections

From time to time you'll find that you're not moving in the right direction. Much as you learned in "Follow Your Own Guidance," when you're off course, you need to make a minor (or sometimes major) course correction. If Ben is in Florida and he wants to drive to New York, he can get in his car and drive. If he has a map, he can estimate how long it will take to get to New York. He'll probably make minor corrections, such as taking a different road, but he'll keep moving towards New York. If Ben is going in the wrong direction, heading south instead of north, he'll hit the ocean instead.

Obviously, the sooner you realize that you're "heading in the wrong direction" the sooner you can make a course correction. Assuming you started out with little or no knowledge of your topic, you might make significant progress in the wrong direction before you realize it. Let your judgment system guide you and don't be afraid to make major directional changes. Even if you're sure that you're going the right way, don't assume you will stay on course. If you become too rigid in your thinking you may avoid making regular and necessary judgments.

Revising Your Goals

Let's say Ben is on his way from Florida to New York, heading north, making great time. He estimates that he'll be there in two days. All of these things would indicate that he's moving toward his goal. He knows how close he is to New York and how much farther he must travel to get there. He merely has to drive in the same direction for another two days. At the end of the first day Ben suddenly decides that he doesn't want to go to New York, even though he's already halfway there. Should he go to New York anyway, even though he doesn't want to? Or should he turn around and go back to Florida? Common sense tells him to turn around and go back, but some people would hesitate to change their plans if they were partway there and significant effort was involved in going back. To them, sticking to the original plan would be easier. What they don't realize is that their productivity level drops to zero the moment they decided to continue in a direction that no longer holds their interest.

At some point in your life you may face changes in your desires. What should you do when you no longer want what you wanted before? If the momentum of many years carried you in that direction, it may take considerable effort to change your direction. A goal that you clearly do not want is not worth pursuing, especially when it prevents you from pursuing other goals that you do want. Don't be afraid to make major changes in life, even if it means dropping something that you decide is no longer desirable.

Before you drop a goal, make sure that you really don't want to pursue it. There will be times when you feel as if the work required to achieve a goal is too much and you don't want to do it. You may still want to achieve the goal, but when you are overwhelmed, mere discomfort may feel like actual disinterest. Let's go back to Ben's New York example. Even though he hates making the long drive, he still wants to go to New York. Instead of driving to New York, Ben takes an airplane. Don't fall into the trap of cutting out a worthy objective, when it may be just a part of the process you don't want to endure. Try changing the process.

Have Fun

Fun keeps you interested, and it prevents your project from becoming a chore and hampering your progress. Judge whether or not you are having fun. If you are having fun, that's great. If you're not, take a break and do something you enjoy. It will re-energize you. What you do for fun can be very simple. If you've learned a few chords on the piano, write a one-verse song using just those chords. If you're learning a new language, watch a TV program or listen to a tape in that language and try to pick out the recognizable words and phrases. If you're learning about your new computer, try to draw a picture, or print out your motto in fancy fonts. If it feels like a reward to you for a job well done, then it must be fun.

14 Ten-Point Review

B y now you should be well acquainted with the ten points of *The Ultimate Lesson*. To learn on your own and advance at your own pace, let them work together. Let's review each of the points and remember, they are all equally important.

1. Find the Incentive

You've learned the importance of goal-setting and how it leads you in the right direction. Set powerful and motivating goals for yourself and make sure you really want each one. Have fun throughout the process, but be careful not to focus only on the end reward. If the process itself frustrates you, the goal might not be worth the trouble. Furthermore, don't set goals that involve doing something you don't like to do merely to avoid doing something else later. Think in terms of doing rather than "being."

Keep a clear view of your potential payoff. Make sure it's a reward, tangible or intangible, that will indicate when you have "won the game," so to speak. Some of your payoffs will be short-term, and others will be long-term. Think long-term, but allow yourself to achieve interim goals so you will get small rewards along the way. They'll also indicate your progress. Define your own reality and pay no attention to negative-thinking people who want to destroy your dreams. Avoid adopting their view of what is "realistic."

Set up motivational and inspirational incentives that relate to your goals to keep yourself moving forward. Don't be afraid to use negative motivation to keep yourself away from something you don't want. Link fear to the failure to achieve your goals. Do everything you can to unlearn the mundane and uninspired learning methods that were forced upon you in traditional school.

2. Enforce The Belief

Remember that beliefs and fears are learned behaviors and they can be unlearned. There are many real fears, however, that should remain a part of your natural defense system. It is more important to identify and rid yourself of the false fears that you somehow adopted over the course of your life. These fears stop you from doing what you dream of or making the changes necessary to achieve your goals and dreams. Form your own empowering labels about yourself and avoid limiting labels. Don't think of yourself as being only left- or right-brained, think of yourself as both. Remember that your future has no limits, and it isn't predicted by your past just because you once behaved a certain way or failed to achieve what you wanted. Your future is limited only by the imaginary roadblocks that you place in your own path.

Use the beliefs that you already have to help construct your new empowering beliefs. Build a productive belief stage by stage, starting at the lowest level. Add a productive fear the same way. Dismantle your limiting beliefs and fears, and watch out for the fear of success, the demon that sabotages you. Destroy the fear of failure and refuse to let it prevent you from taking action.

3. Follow Your Own Guidance

You'll need a hat rack for the two new hats you'll be wearing. You're the student and you're also the teacher. If you always keep your objective in mind, you'll know what steps must be taken to reach your destination. Focus on your goal and allow it to help you find where to begin. Remember, you don't always have to start right at the beginning, wherever that may be. You can make significant progress by starting in an area that is familiar or fun. When you begin with the part of a subject that is most enjoyable, it will motivate you to continue.

Use your teacher's hat to help select the learning materials you'll need. Buy or borrow study guides, non-study guides, and other supporting materials relating to your subject. You'll also need the related equipment that allows you to practice whatever it is that you're learning. If you're learning a musical instrument, get that instrument. Supporting equipment, like a computer, can be a great help, too. Utilize the materials and equipment that allow you to learn in the most effective manner. Some people learn best by reading books, while others learn well by listening or watching. Everyone learns best by doing something related to the particular subject they're studying.

Constantly monitor your direction. Point yourself in the general direction of your destination, but be prepared to make course corrections when you need to. Keep tabs on your final goal too. As you make progress, be sure that you're enjoying the work. As you learn more about what achieving your goal will bring about, make sure that you still want it. Identify the wrong course early, and don't finish a project just because you started it if it's no longer desirable.

Chances are good that you'll be able to find a mentor who has experience in your field of interest. Your mentor can be someone you know or someone you don't know, a famous person, or someone who is no longer living. Do a little research and find out everything you can about your mentor. Apply your mentor's experience to what you've already learned for yourself. Watch mentors in non-related fields too, because they can be an additional source of inspiration.

4. Begin With Small Steps

You learn much more by doing something than by simply reading or hearing about it. Throw yourself into your subject and put pressure on your intellect to keep growing, much like weightlifters build their muscles. If it is uncomfortable at first, don't give up, just keep doing it. Your subject will gradually become natural, until little or no conscious thinking is involved. Take small steps to slowly build up to this level. Don't push your intellect beyond its ability to understand in a rush for speed and progress. Once the mind understands a procedure or action, it stores that "program" and subconsciously runs it when called for. The more often a program is run and fine tuned, the more smoothly it operates. Steady repetition and naturally increasing speed will help your mind master the "program" after a relatively short time period. Be conscious of everything you're learning, whether it's history, karate, mathematics or gardening. Allow your confidence to flow into other areas of your subject or into other subjects as well.

To begin a project, take a small step that you're relatively certain you can successfully complete. That first step may be significant or it may be microscopic. Whatever it is, allow yourself to feel a sense of accomplishment, then build the confidence you attain from this mini-success into the belief that you can master the subject in its entirety. Interpret your learning at the highest level by reminding yourself that you've learned something on your own, so you can learn something else on your own as well. As a confidence-building exercise, take further steps in subjects that you're already familiar with, and complete simple steps in new subjects. Use all of this as ammunition to blast yourself past the intimidating size of large projects.

As you grow you'll steadily increase the size of the steps you're taking. Increase the size of your steps at a natural pace. If you always keep a little pressure on yourself you'll stimulate your growth. Don't put so much stress on yourself that you give up. Recognize and congratulate yourself every time you reach a new plateau. Let your confidence grow in both your subject and the self-learning process.

5. Learn From Your Mistakes

The principle of trial and error has given us the electric light bulb, the television set, and virtually every other useful product or invention since the discovery of fire. You'll learn ten times more from your mistakes than you will from your successes. Some mistakes will be obvious, sometimes shockingly so, and will stay with you forever. Don't make the same mistake twice. Be on the lookout for the obscure mistakes as well. Sometimes the results of an obscure mistake won't be seen for a long time. The longer you go before identifying your mistake, the more effort it will require to correct.

Be aggressive in searching for the root of the mistake and do whatever it takes to get to the bottom of it. Carefully analyze incorrect results and make sure you identify where you took the wrong turn. Remember that it isn't always the actions you took right before the current results that may have caused those results. It may have been from an action you took much earlier.

Always maintain your safety net. Be absolutely certain that you're familiar with the risks of your undertaking and be sure that you can live with the worst possible outcome. Be aware that you simply cannot afford to make mistakes that will endanger anyone. Don't attempt to learn anything on your own where a mistake could result in harm to yourself or anyone else.

6. Use Patterns

Look for similarities and patterns on a small scale and utilize them in other areas of your subject. The easiest patterns to use are distinctive. They repeat regularly and can be transposed in a wide variety of ways. They range from a chord on the piano keyboard to the step-by-step procedure for building a house. These can clearly be followed, and they don't change very much no matter where you use them. They are also the patterns that will be of the most use to you. The obscure patterns, such as economic trends or human behavior, are a little harder to follow and somewhat more difficult to predict. The further disadvantage of these types of patterns is that there is no guarantee that they'll repeat. If a vague or obscure pattern relates to your subject, it can give you some valuable insight if you are able to break it down.

Dissect the pattern and aggressively seek out its roots. Sometimes a pattern's foundation will be hard to see, but it will be there for you to find if you search hard enough. Look for the simplest recognizable elements. Look for smaller patterns within a larger pattern. Once you have recognized a pattern, experiment by placing it over other foundations of your subject. Use the trial-and-error process to see which patterns work where and keep a mental log of what works and what doesn't.

7. Adapt to the Requirements

Your mind and body automatically condition themselves to handle just about anything that is thrown at them. This is often a natural reflex action that occurs with little or no conscious thought. People who were born with severe disadvantages have no choice but to adapt. By default they reach a stage where they "naturally" perform tasks that seem to be impossible to a normal person. Normal people don't have the incentive to adapt in such ways. If we set ourselves up in a way that forces us to adapt, we'll do so.

Adaptation is growth occurring from cycles of stress followed by cycles of recovery. After exertion, the mind and the body must rest and recover. This is where growth and adaptation take place. If you continually stress your mind and body without allowing them a recovery period, there will be little chance for any growth. If you feel that you're having trouble adapting, it could be that you're not allowing yourself enough of a recovery period.

If you want to stimulate your adaptation skills, try different approaches. Look over what you've accomplished so far, and if you haven't yet reached that level where your work feels like second nature, work at it a little more and you'll get there. Try taking smaller steps or skipping ahead a little. Let your subject excite you and set new interim goals that will inspire you along the way. Look at how fast you're adapting and look for signs that you're holding yourself back.

8. Overcome the Obstacles

Fear stops more people from being successful than just about anything else. The fears that will stop you are generally not fears of physical safety or pain. Most of them relate to the unknown or to change. There's little reason to fear the unknown, or to fear change. Dismantle these fears using the principles found under "Enforce the Belief." Recognize that your fear is a mental roadblock, and learn to hate it. Make a pledge with yourself to destroy your fear at all costs.

Since you enjoy doing what feels natural, and since one of your goals is to reach the level where your activities feel natural, you will probably have to pass through some level of discomfort. If you're doing something that feels a little uncomfortable you're probably developing your learning skills. Associate the joy of knowing you've advanced with your discomfort, but make sure it's taking you in the right direction. When you reach a level of frustration where you can't go any further, take a short break. Allow yourself the satisfaction of knowing that you've gotten the most out of yourself. After you recover and try again, you'll get even better results.

Disbelief is another mental obstacle that must be dealt with and dismantled. As a diversion, try learning something that is simple and fun. Re-emphasize your goals and take a few small steps to gain confidence. Motivate yourself by watching some of the winners in your field and remove all disbelief from your mind.

Treat physical obstacles as you would treat mental obstacles. If you look at them from a different perspective they can become less intimidating. If you believe you're lacking equipment or money, try reducing your initial requirements. Forget about the myths of age. Refuse to believe that you are too old or too young to do anything. If you think you lack the physical ability to do something, review the section on mental obstacles.

9. Fill In the Gaps

The missing pieces of your subject will show themselves with a little prodding. When you come across something that you don't understand, chances are one or more of the significant supporting elements is missing. Never believe that you lack the ability to understand something. Instead, know that you may have missed a key segment of the foundation. If necessary, backtrack until you reach the level where you understand your subject again. Ask yourself questions and break down each part of your subject as you gradually identify the missing parts. Sometimes just identifying a missing part will make other parts of the material more understandable.

As you search for these missing parts keep your eye on the sequence in which you take the steps to achieve your goal. Many tasks must be learned or performed in a certain order. For instance, you wouldn't paint the walls of a house before the walls are nailed into place and plastered. When you don't understand part of a subject or you are unable to move forward on a project, it may be the result of an improper sequence. You may have to dig for information or experiment a little to find the right sequence. Learn from your mistakes, and you'll eventually find the proper sequence.

10. Judge the Results

To judge your own results, you'll need to put on your teacher's hat again. Knowing your objective is the critical factor here. As long as you know what you want to achieve, you can critically evaluate your progress. Continue to ask yourself if your methods are working properly, and note the progress you're making. Does this progress satisfy you or do you need to push harder? Try to ensure that you're still having fun and don't forget to give yourself interim rewards along the way.

Use the self-judgment system to determine course corrections that may be necessary for continued success and to reach your ultimate destination. It's important to make significant course corrections if they're called for. If you find that any part of your original goal no longer suits you, don't hesitate to revise it.

Let the Ten Points Work Together

The ten points of *The Ultimate Lesson* should all be used together. Commit them to memory and keep them at the forefront of your mind as you attack each and every new subject. If you can keep your eye on the reward, push yourself, and have fun along the way, there are very few subjects that you cannot master. You'll be amazed at the results you can achieve, and your confidence will grow at an extraordinary rate. After you learn the first skill on your own, every subsequent skill will be twice as easy to master. It won't be long before you become a master of the self-learning process. You'll have the confidence and courage to take on challenges that you never dreamed were possible.

15 Applying Your Ability

Learning a New Skill

Now that you've armed yourself with the powerful self-learning ability, select the first subject or skill that you want to teach yourself. You've learned how to set motivating goals and how to keep your objective in mind to motivate you through the self-learning process. There are literally thousands of subjects from which you can chose. Chose something that you enjoy as your first challenge. If it's something fun, you'll have a leg up from the start.

Throughout this book I have consistently used the examples of music, language, business, construction, and sports. These general subjects alone give us hundreds of possibilities; however, in no way should you let this limit your thinking. You can take on any subject or challenge with complete confidence that you can master it. There are as many different reasons for doing something as there are subjects to learn. You may be looking for personal advancement, increased income, more fun, or merely an ego boost. Let's take a look at a few diverse subjects and how you might approach them. Remember, you should have a strong interest in any subject you approach.

A car buff wants to live out his fantasy of rebuilding an old Austin-Healy sports car. Fred isn't a trained mechanic, but because of his interest in cars he has read a great deal about cars over the years and knows how a car operates. He's also read about different models of cars, vintages, and market values. Fred's motivation was part passion for cars and part desire to rebuild a car and sell it for a profit. After finding the Austin-Healy, he takes it home, opens the hood, and looks inside. He quickly recognizes the radiator, the carburetor, the spark plugs, the transmission, and all of the other parts he's been reading about. Fred drives his new car around with his senses alert to identify problems, then he parks it in his garage and disassembles the engine. As he takes things apart, he carefully looks at how each of the parts are put together, and how the parts work together as a whole. He's done a little research and got his hands on a manual for the Austin-Healy. One by one Fred identifies the smallest parts that need replacement or repair. He has never seen some of the parts before, but he's learning about them as he goes. Then he puts the car back together one piece at a time. This part goes a little slower, but Fred has his manual to help guide him. He's learning more than anyone could by just reading a book. Later he installs new tires, puts on a fresh coat of paint, and shows it off. A process like this could be as short as a month or as long as two years, depending upon the amount of time a person has to devote.

When I was growing up we had a 1966 Mustang convertible. In the early '80s it was rusted and falling apart. We sold it for about $1,000 to someone like Fred. He was young and it was his first car. We saw him about a year later, and he had rebuilt the car so thoroughly that we didn't even recognize it. He later sold it for more than $10,000.

One of the first events I ever organized was a go-cart race. Every year young racers would bring their home-built, non-motorized go-carts to race down the hill near my house. The top competitors of the various races would get gold, silver, and bronze medals. The overall winner would get a trophy, some local newspaper coverage, and occasionally a TV appearance. It was similar to the well-known Soap Box Derby except there were absolutely no rules on how the go-carts had to be constructed. The races coupled straight-ahead downhill racing with slalom courses. To win the overall prize, a racer had to be competitive in both areas. One year we had a young man about nine years of age who, with his father's help, had build a rather large go-cart that was impressively fast. That year I gave him gold medals in all of the downhill races just because his go-cart was so much faster than the others. Unfortunately, his go-cart didn't turn very well and he was unable to compete in the slalom races. To this day I clearly remember how disappointed he was when I awarded the grand prize to someone else.

When the following year's event came, so did our young man with the same go-cart. When I said hello, he told me that he was going to win the grand prize that day. I admired his ambition and wished him good luck. As I announced the names of the competitors, I noticed that our young man's name was on the list for the slalom races as well as the downhill races. Remembering that his go-cart couldn't turn very well the previous year, I feared that he would crash if he attempted the slalom events. I asked him and his father to come to the side to discuss it, but his father assured me that it would be all right. His run at the slalom was stunning. He turned on a dime and made two consecutive perfect runs in record time. He had rebuilt the steering system specifically for competition in the slalom races. He took home five gold medals and the grand prize trophy that day, just as he had said he would. A week later he joined me for a TV interview. He told the entire city of Boston that the moment he was defeated the year before, his goal to win became a true driving force. He had identified the obstacles and adapted to achieve his goal. He now runs a successful construction business.

Advancing at Work

Everyone wants to get ahead at work. You're looking for that promotion, an increase in salary and status, or perhaps even to run the company one day. You'll have endless opportunities to advance by learning on your own, and other times where advancement may be difficult, if not impossible, without it.

Do you work for a large corporation, and do you know what your boss wants? Does he want you to make some breakthrough sale or a discovery that will be good for the company? Is he going out of his way to help you rise up the corporate ladder? He may want you to keep quiet and not stir things up. At the same time he wants to take credit for your good work and get promoted himself. In environments like this, initiative often goes without reward and quickly dies, along with an employee's passion and excitement for their job. A common piece of advice to you from a boss or a co-worker who is stuck in this environment is "don't rock the boat" or "don't make waves." If you adhere to this philosophy the only force that will move you is the drifting tide.

Suppose you get brave (or bored) and decide to rock the boat anyway. You have a great idea which you think will be effective for helping your department perform better. If you ask permission first, you're sure you'll be turned down. So without asking, you try it anyway. It works well, but your boss yells at you for not asking his permission. Welcome his attention, because now you can point out to him that it's going to make him look good as well. Perhaps both of you will rise through the ranks of the company as a result. On the other hand, what if your idea hadn't turned out so well? You're going to get yelled at for sure, and you might get fired. How much damage did you really do to the company, and how much did you learn from doing it?

I once heard a story about a very understanding CEO. It seems one of his senior employees made a series of poor decisions that cost the company close to ten million dollars. When he was called into the CEO's office the executive said, "I expect you want me to resign."

"Certainly not," said the CEO. "We've just spent ten million dollars on your education."

It's obviously unwise to risk losing a significant amount of your company's money without permission. That is good grounds for getting fired. However, if you minimize the risk to the company so that the potential loss is small, your superiors may look more favorably upon your initiative.

Many large companies are quite bureaucratic and in such companies employees at all levels struggle to justify their existence. It's been said that many employees rise to their own level of incompetence. As they get promoted up the chain, their job description changes drastically. Just because someone is proficient in sales, for example, doesn't mean that he will make a good sales manager, nor does it mean that he would want that job. Many bosses are constantly running scared. They don't always welcome hotshot employees fast on their tail who could have their job or get promoted ahead of them.

Learn your boss's job anyway. It's a logical promotion for you, and the boss is right there to learn from. It's not too hard to watch what she does every day and get a good idea of how to do her job. If she's secure in her position and ripe for a promotion herself, she may welcome the help you give her. If, on the other hand, she knows she has reached the highest job she's ever going to have, she may try to fire you or sabotage your efforts to get ahead. Tread carefully.

Perhaps you work in one division of a company but your real passion is for a different division. You know it because you walk by every day and see people doing the job you want to do. This is particularly true in the entertainment business. People are desperate to get in at any level. They often start by taking a job in the mailroom of a movie studio or talent agency. After a year or two in the mailroom, a small percentage of those who "had what it took" manage to finagle their way into an assistant position for a high-level executive or agent. While in this position they're subjected to long, stressful hours of work, catering to every need and whim of their boss. At night the assistants read movie scripts, have meetings, and often behave as if they're the bosses. The people who do this successfully get results (which can be in the form of one single deal) and are often promoted. Now the people working in the mailroom want to work for the newly promoted employee. And the cycle continues.

I once had a low-level job in the music business. I was the assistant to a high-level music executive. I took very good care of him and at the same time learned a great deal about the music industry. With the help of what I learned when I worked for him I later produced, promoted and distributed the debut album featuring my rock band, Veronica's Toy.

When I was in the Air Force in the early '80s, I worked at the radio and TV station of an air base in the Middle East. I started in the radio department, but I really wanted to do TV news. They told me they had no plans to move me into the news department during my one-year tour, but in my spare time I helped in the news department anyway. I even produced news reports on my own. They welcomed the help and eventually put me in the news department just as I had wanted.

If you want to move up in a company, large or small, think like an owner. Even if you're in a low-level supporting position, with little or no direct connection to the main part of the business, try to become intimate with the company's core product or service, even if you have to do it in your spare time. An owner knows what the company does, what it sells, and how it operates. The owner also realizes that he is in command and nobody else is there to tell him what to do. If he doesn't get it right, he could lose his business.

Building a Business

The thought of owning and operating your own business, reaping rewards from the work, and above all being your own boss is tantalizing. Many people dream of such an entrepreneurial opportunity. Here is where self-learners can utilize all of their talents and flourish.

What exactly does an entrepreneur do? An entrepreneur finds a need for a product or service and fills it at an acceptable price. Some of the greatest business successes are people who were once faced with the need for something that didn't exist. White-out, the correcting fluid that secretaries use to touch up typing mistakes, was invented by a secretary. In the days before computers and copy machines, multiple copies of documents had to be typed with carbon paper. If a mistake was made, all of the copies had to be retyped. This particular secretary wanted to avoid the tedious retyping process so she tried mixing clear nail polish with flour. The result was an opaque white liquid that covered the mistakes and then dried. She later became a multimillionaire and retired from her secretarial position.

The right idea for starting a business will sometimes just hit you, often when you least expect it. Observe everything you possibly can during your day-to-day activities. What frustrates you? What do you wish you had that doesn't exist? What do other people wish they had that doesn't exist? Whenever you feel like muttering "someone should invent..." chances are you've hit upon a good possibility. After this happens a number of times, you may come up with a very good idea. If nobody else has thought of it and, to your knowledge, the market is wide open, then go for it. The idea for this book came to me when I was in the shower.

What is the right business for you? It should be a type of business you enjoy. Your good idea for a new product doesn't guarantee that you'll enjoy producing and marketing it, unless that's what you love to do. If you're a sports buff, for example, you might not enjoy inventing some sort of a bathroom aid. Again, don't set out to do something just for the money.

Once your idea is firm, it's time to use your newfound self-learning prowess. For this example, let's say you've decided to create and market a simple product. You've figured out how to make a prototype, so you start absorbing as much information as you can about production, sales, marketing, and generally running a business. First, think like your customer. Who is he or she? Why is this customer going to buy your product over another product? How will they purchase it? How will you make the customer aware of your product? If it is sold in stores, how will it get to the stores? If you start at the customer level and detail every step of the process all the way back to the prototype, you will uncover a wealth of knowledge on how to bring your product to the market.

Keep your business small to start. It will grow at its own pace. It's easier to start a business selling small products by mail order from your home than to start an electronics manufacturing plant. As a general rule, the more money required to start, the less control and equity the founder retains.

The person who's only the inventor and doesn't care to know much about business will probably not be as successful as someone who takes the time to learn each part of the business from the ground up. Much like the teacher/student role you play as you teach yourself, you will be doing nearly all the jobs in your business at first. Try each hat on for size. One day you'll be the production supervisor and another day you may be the marketing manager. Later you might be the finance officer, or the chief salesman. This experience with different jobs is an opportunity to learn how to operate the whole business. Furthermore, when you do take on employees and delegate important tasks, you'll be capable of supervising them and maintaining an accurate overview of the situation.

Hopefully you'll make massive sales and your product will be a hit. You'd think this positive motivation would be enough, but don't forget the other side of the coin. Once you've started, it's possible that you could lose a significant amount of money if your business fails. As soon as you put something valuable at risk, the fear of losing it will compel you to work harder to make even more progress. The hope for a large financial reward isn't always as powerful a motivator as the fear of a large financial loss. Make your fear work for you. Let it push you to action if you ever feel you're getting a little lazy or too comfortable.

As your business grows you'll hire employees. Hire people who are interested in doing the work, not just making money, and delegate important tasks to them quickly. Throw them into the fire just as you did yourself. In addition, delegate self-learning to them. Encourage them to take risks (while you retain responsibility and control) to help grow with the company and advance in their particular department or division. Imagine the impact on your business if every one of your staff utilized their own self-learning ability. Your business will grow and the rewards will be unlimited.

Productive Play

In the park near my home in Los Angeles a fairly intense basketball game takes place every Sunday morning. I don't play much basketball myself, but on occasion I watch for a few minutes after a morning run. You'd think this weekend basketball game would be fun and light-hearted, but these guys play like the NBA championship was at stake. There's plenty of pushing, yelling, scream-ing, personal fouls, and even some chair-throwing. It doesn't look as if it's very enjoyable, but after it's over everyone is laughing.

It's clear that these weekend warriors have fun playing and there's no doubt they love the game. As everyone knows, the more you practice the better you get. As in the tennis example earlier, you can teach yourself a sport as soon as you know the rules and get the proper equip-ment. These players will practice shooting the ball for hours on their own and play a little one-on-one whenever they get the chance. They must constantly improve if they want to continue to play in this high-level weekend game.

From fly-fishing to knitting to skydiving, we all love our recreational activities. We taught ourselves the skills in those recreational activities. How did we do it? First, we had a strong desire to learn, and second, learning it was fun. The more you do it, the better you get, but if you do something fun, you'll get even better.

The point is that we all have self-learning ability. If we can learn a recreational activity by ourselves, we can learn anything by ourselves. If you meet someone who doubts their self-learning ability, ask them what they do for fun, then ask them how they learned to do it. Point out the self learning principle whenever you see it in someone else.

Keep reminding yourself of this, and remember that anytime you do something you enjoy you're probably getting better at it. This is your self-learning ability in action. When you're fully conscious of it, it will grow and give you increasing confidence in all other areas and subjects.

From Parent to Child

You're never too old or too young to benefit from self-learning. Learning to walk is a child's first experience in self-learning. It shapes the child's life until he is "taught" to do it another way. Since he's never been told not to, the child will explore the things he imagines will be fun. If he gets a new toy he manipulates it until he gets a result that he likes. After that he knows just what to do to get that particular result.

As the child gets older and his communication skills improve, the parent will get a better idea of what he enjoys. His activities, so long as they are not destructive, should be encouraged but not pushed. If you push something on a child he'll probably lose interest in it even if he enjoys it. If this loss of interest is caused by too much pressure from a parent, recovery will be very difficult. A negative image is now associated with the activity, and he loses sight of the fun.

A growing child needs exposure to as many different things as possible. Football fans who watch the weekend game and throw empty beer cans at the TV are created at an early age when a child wants to be "just like dad." On the other hand, a father can create a good work ethic in his son if he can make working in the yard, or doing other mundane chores, more enjoyable. Maybe the child won't enjoy everything, but the reward of a cold drink when the job is done and bonding with Dad may be the right motivation. In the novel *The Adventures of Tom Sawyer*, young Tom got the other kids to paint the fence by convincing them that the process was fun.

Show your children something fun and then let them alone to have fun with it. If you play the piano and your child enjoys it, make sure the piano room is accessible. Eventually you will hear some sort of sound originating from that room. Again, encourage but don't push. The results can be astounding.

As the child continues to do things on her own, she builds her confidence in her self-learning ability. The more her parents allow her to develop naturally, the less likely it is that she will lose her self-learning ability as she goes through traditional school. Keep giving her new challenges to learn on her own and with practice her self-learning ability will be useful to her for life. Nobody will be able to take it away from her.

In Times of Crisis

Crisis presents the greatest self-learning opportunity of them all. It's also the most important time to fully utilize that ability. When the chips are down and everything is crashing around you, what do you do? Do you give up? What happens if you give up? You might lose everything you've worked for. Your natural instinct is to not let this happen.

Once you've made up your mind that you are not going down without a fight, your self-learning ability will automatically shift into high gear. To fully recover you may have to do things you never planned to do, and learn things you never planned to learn. You may not enjoy all of the process, but the alternative is always worse. Hopefully, your fear of that negative alternative will push you to succeed.

A small factory was purchased by a larger company. The factory employed one hundred and fifty people who produced a few simple products. It was marginally profitable but not very efficient. The former CEO of the factory had recently retired and the operation lacked effective leadership. Furthermore, the factory was on valuable land. The new company planned to close and demolish the factory to make way for lucrative residential housing. An executive from the new company held a meeting with the department heads and gave them the bad news. When they heard that the factory would be shut down, the department heads were jolted into action. They'd had it too easy for too long.

Fortunately one of the department heads had a good bit of fire in his belly. James took over leadership of the factory and then met with the head of the company that planned to shut them down. The boss explained the situation to James in greater detail. Unless the factory became significantly more profitable, it wouldn't make economic sense to keep it operating. James didn't leave the office without getting a commitment from the boss that he would keep the factory operating if certain goals were met within a six-month period.

Upon his return to the factory, James met with the other department heads again. He told them that they would have to triple their production or they would lose their jobs. They all thought he was crazy. None of them believed they could do it.

"I don't think you understand," said James. "Unless we meet all of these goals and more, the factory will be shut down in six months and all of us will be looking for work." This message was communicated down the chain of command like a lightning bolt. Everybody knew that if they didn't produce fast they would all be unemployed. It was the factory's most desperate hour.

The desperation worked. They employees rallied like never before. At the end of six months they had quadrupled their output, and instead of shutting the factory down the company modernized the factory and gave significant bonuses to all the employees.

Lee Iacocca, the famous automotive executive, had an illustrious career at the Ford Motor Company. He rose to the position of president until the chairman, Henry Ford II, fired him under rather bitter conditions. Iacocca was devastated. Then the Chrysler Corporation, in the midst of severe financial trouble, came knocking at Iacocca's door. They needed a complete turnaround and they wanted to install him as president. Iacocca already had enough money to retire. He thought about it, but didn't really want to go through the turmoil and difficulty required to turn Chrysler around. His wife said, "I bet Mr. Ford would love to hear that." That was all it took for Iacocca to accept the job and lead Chrysler through one of the most spectacular turnarounds in American corporate history.

Why do we behave this way? The hope of winning can be outweighed by the fear of losing. At this stage of the game the help and guidance available from others is scarce. We must learn on our own how to recover from impending disaster.

When we realize that we're in trouble it's time to analyze and assess the situation. The first day Iacocca went into Chrysler, he had no idea what they needed. He had to find out what was broken before he could fix it. If you walked into a doctor's office with an ailment and he gave you a prescription without thoroughly examining you, would you take the medicine? Probably not. You'd have little confidence in the diagnosis. A doctor must find out exactly what's wrong with a patient before prescribing medicine or recommending treatment. We must do this too. A thorough diagnosis of our situation will lead us toward the right solution.

In times of crisis, we learn a great deal more about ourselves and our situation. We come up with ideas to change the situation to benefit us, but there will be significant trial and error in the process. As you recover from a crisis you should actively seek solutions. You will usually find whatever you focus on, whether you are looking for a problem or a solution. Attorneys are good at this. If a client calls up and says "I've signed a contract that I shouldn't have signed, get me out of it," an attorney will read the contract, looking for problems, flaws, and ultimately a way out. They usually find a loophole and send a form letter stating that the contract is invalid for one reason or another.

As you work your way out of a crisis, focus on solving the problem. You will also be gathering information to help keep you out of this particular situation in the future. In most cases you'll automatically avoid the activities that brought you into the crisis in the first place.

16 The Future of Traditional Education

Affordable Education is Coming

What happens to a student who endures the sweat and agony of earning a degree from a top business school? If she graduates near the top of her class she may be recruited by a large corporation. What did it cost her? Tuition fees are going up by thousands of dollars every year. Even with school loans readily available, a professional education may soon be out of the price range of students who don't have a rich family. Graduate students often seek a large salary but are very lucky to find an initial job that pays close to what they expect. It is usually several years before sig-

161

nificant raises are offered. When I was a legal assistant, one of the young attorneys I worked for took home less money than I did. With living expenses and those hefty student loan payments you might start to question the value of a graduate degree that is supposed to make your life easier.

Undergraduates face an even tougher challenge. These poor souls get dropped into the real world at 22 years old, straight out of college, with little or no life experience. It isn't the most desirable position to be in during a job interview. You need experience to get a job, and nobody will give you a job if you don't have previous experience. Why should a company give an inexperienced person the job when they can choose someone who took the initiative to go out and get some experience on their own?

Everyone needs school to learn the basics of language, math, and science, but what is the actual value of a college degree? Let's say a basic undergraduate degree from the smallest and least expensive of city colleges costs around $10,000. To find out if it is worth that much the law of supply and demand must be considered. You've paid $10,000 for some information; however, most of it is available for a small fraction of the cost or in some cases for free. Text books, on-line databases, and many other sources can be used to gather the same information that you'd get from attending college. It may just require a little more time and effort to organize. The same principle is true for a business degree. Virtually all of the information available through a college business program is available to the general public for little or no cost in one form or another. Again, you'll have to research and assemble it yourself.

Most people purchase a college degree for two reasons: for the information they think they cannot get anywhere else, and because they believe it will guarantee them a good job. The large and sometimes rather stale corporations of America do believe that a person with a degree from an upscale university is acceptable. However, the world is full of people who were excellent scholars but don't know which way is up in the real world. Then there are those who drop out of high school and later become millionaires. Formal education isn't a guarantee of success, and a lack of formal education isn't a guarantee of failure, but the "guaranteed employment" theory of a college degree can go in the round file.

Most students mistakenly believe that the skills they learn in college will be in demand for the rest of their working lifetime and that good jobs will come looking for them. If you can get all the information yourself, and a job is not guaranteed, then what are you really buying with the money you pay to a university for a degree? Is it worth the money just to have the information assembled and presented to you? Certainly not.

I do believe that college degrees have significant value and I am not saying it is a waste of time to get one. If you can afford it, then by all means go for it. There are many jobs for which a formal education can increase the chances of success. I only mention this theory to illustrate a couple of points. One, education is available to virtually everyone; and two, the actual cost of obtaining the knowledge is truly affordable.

It is wrong to think that only the rich people can obtain a "superior" education. Computers with modems are now making information exchange easy. One of the new popular buzzwords in the business world is telecommuting. People work from home and simply "log in" to the office. At the end of the day they "log out." They save an incredible amount of time because they avoid the daily round trip to and from the office.

You can get an education with the same kind of efficiency at home on a computer. We'll refer to this as "tele-learning." Why pay for expensive facilities and professors when you can have access to all the information you need at home? You can also work and learn at your own pace. If you cannot afford to buy a computer, some libraries have computers on-line, and offer their use to the public for a small fee.

There are a handful of formal on-line educational materials available already. All major universities now have Internet sites. The University of Phoenix offers an on-line MBA degree among other programs. Computers are widely recognized as a business tool, but they have just begun to be recognized as a powerful educational tool. Computer technology goes through revolutions every few years. We're currently in the midst of a revolution that is linking the countries of the world through the information superhighway. I believe that the next great revolution in computers will be that of on-line formal education and self-learning educational software. I also believe that within five to ten years the true cost of a college-level education (with all of the information properly assembled) will be little more than the cost of a single CD-ROM, available to virtually everyone.

Is all of this acceptable? It depends on who you ask. A college degree can be framed and put on a wall. The real test of a person's education and knowledge is a job well done. If a corporation wants to stay ahead in the game it must aggressively recruit people who can do the job, not just college graduates who figuratively fit the bill. You know now that the key to success in life is on-going self-education. People who continually self-learn will be qualified for new jobs based on their abilities. The companies of tomorrow will take chances on self-educated employees and promote them as their true value becomes evident.

17 The Ongoing Challenge

Be a Self-Starter

Everyone is born with the potential for genius. Children have infinite self-learning capability. As we grow up, however, we become more vulnerable to believing that we're dependent upon others. This is clearly a false belief. We've seen that self-learning is simple and natural. We've identified many areas of life in which you've already used it. If you ever get stuck, go back through the ten points of *The Ultimate Lesson*. Most likely one of them will help you break through any barrier. You can accomplish anything unless you allow yourself to be convinced otherwise.

The incentive for personal growth falls upon your shoulders. If you're looking for assistance and guidance it's out there, but others' desire to help you won't be nearly as strong as your own. This isn't to say that everyone is selfish, but others are probably looking to help themselves first.

The more you practice self-learning, the better you'll get. Soon it will take you less time to learn and you'll have the confidence to take on increasingly difficult challenges. Commit yourself to learning at least one new skill every year. This can be something productive and profitable, or it can be something fun that you've always wanted to do. If you keep learning, imagine where you'll be at the end of five years, then ten years, and so on.

Your self-learning is unique to you, just as others' self-learning is unique to them. As you've learned, this ability is simply a form of awareness. It isn't a complicated method that must be memorized, nor is it reserved for those who have "superior intelligence." Your friends and associates may be in awe and amazement of your progress. Teach them what you have learned, and show them what you have accomplished—not to impress them, but to inspire and share the wealth with them. Help them unlock their own self-learning ability and you'll form many lifelong, fulfilling relationships.

What Now?

That's the million-dollar question. With thousands of subjects to choose from, it's difficult to make a single recommendation. Ask yourself where you want to be and what you want to be doing for the next five years. Find out what you really like, and what you don't like. Show me someone who's making a million dollars a year doing what they hate, and someone who makes ten thousand dollars a year doing what they love, and I'll show you a failure and a success. Which is which? If you are ever faced with that option you will know.

Ask questions and allow your answers to guide you in the right direction. Now that you know you can teach yourself anything, use that ability to learn what you love to do. If you continue to love what you're doing, the money and success will follow, and you'll be truly satisfied for a lifetime.

Epilogue: Two Self-Learning Adventures

I've spent the last year or so working on two projects that would not have come together without a great deal of self-learning. This book, of course, was one, and the debut album from my band, Veronica's Toy, was the other. The main thing that they had in common was a clearly identifiable end result together with a highly motivating reward. Both provided numerous obstacles, but both also provided a great deal of satisfaction and fun.

The Ultimate Lesson: The Book

You are holding the end result of what was little more than a distant vision a year ago. The idea for *The Ultimate Lesson* came to me after years of people asking how I learn things without the aid of formal instruction. There was at least one suggestion that I write a book on the subject.

With the idea of writing a book in the back of your head, a walk through the bookstore takes on a whole new meaning. You notice book covers, displays, sales copy on the back of the books, etc. I wanted my book in the stores, so my job was to find out how other books got there. As most of us know there are a number of large book publishers whose names grace the inside of high-profile books. It's also true that hundreds of manuscripts are submitted to these companies each week. Some are good, some are not, some are read, and others are returned with a "thanks, but no thanks" letter. With this in mind, I had a feeling that my proposal might get lost in the shuffle. Even if it did get published, I feared the process might take an extra year or so. For these reasons I decided to self-publish.

I didn't know the first thing about publishing when I started writing, nor had I ever written a book before. I didn't know where to begin at first. Looking back on my first learning experiences with piano and computers, I started thinking about the process I followed to learn them. After organizing those thoughts and identifying the ten *Ultimate Lesson* points, I started thinking about examples of how to illustrate each of them.

There is a certain feeling you get right at the start of a big project. Facing a blank piece of paper knowing that you must write about 200 pages gives you a feeling of just how far you have to go. The first draft took two months of daily 12-hour writing sessions. As I neared the end, I got a rush of energy and often pushed into the wee hours of the morning as the last few sections were coming together. There was a rewarding sense of accomplishment after it was done, but it was quickly replaced with the realization of how much work was yet to come.

I'd had enough writing for a while so I took a little break from the writing process. To keep the project fresh, I gave it to an outside editor for review. At this point, it was time to look more in depth at the subject of actually publishing the book. Through my research, I discovered a book entitled *The Self Publishing Manual* by Dan Poynter. This how-to book was an invaluable source of information and guidance on the subject of self-publishing. It made the process much easier and I'm sure it has saved many people, including myself, a great deal of time.

It was obvious that I would need a printer. Using the directory of printers in the Literary Market Place, I sent out letters to about twenty different printers asking for price quotes. I wasn't sure exactly what to ask for, as I didn't know much about paper and ink. The responses were informative and educational. Through them I learned about "55-pound paper" and "10-point coated one stock." I received some sample books, asked a few questions, and learned quite a bit about printing—things I never would have known had I not been doing a book.

When the book came back from the editor, I was ready with the latest in page design software for my computer. I experimented with different type styles and spacing, and managed to give the layout a nice look. I looked at other books and asked a book designer to review my design. The entire layout process took about a week. Though I'm not a graphic artist, I also took a crack at designing the cover. I had never worked with a computer illustration program before and it took a little effort to get a handle on it. Again, I figured this part of the book could benefit by adding another set of eyes, so I spoke to a graphic designer who offered a few suggestions. It was very exciting to see the concept evolve into the final design. I could see a nearly finished book on the table.

Veronica's Toy: The Debut Album

I've always enjoyed playing the piano. About two years ago a friend took me to a small club to see a local band. They played copy songs (songs made famous by other artists) that the Friday night club audience enjoyed. The band was good, but I was particularly impressed by the singer. He had a powerful voice and always gave a great performance. The band was informal and fun. They often allowed other musicians (or anyone who said they could play an instrument) to sit in for a song or two. One night it was my turn. We played a song that both the band and I knew, and had a blast. Afterward, I spoke with the singer, Tony Gerace, about what he was doing. He told me that he had been playing for a number of years and had been in several bands. While this band was fun, he dreamed of putting together a new band that would do all original music. Somewhere in the back of my mind I had always thought about joining a band, but I had never done it.

That summer, Tony and I started getting together in his garage once a week. I set up my piano, and he pulled out his guitar and a small cassette recorder. We started "jamming" and getting an idea of the kind of music that we liked to play. Tony had the experience of years of live performances and songwriting. He had put out a couple of independent records in his home town of Buffalo, New York. I had never written a song before and the extent of my live performance experience was my few times on stage with Tony's band.

Gradually, we started to write some songs that we thought sounded pretty good. I don't think either one of us knew exactly what we'd do with these but we started to get serious about it. We booked some time in a small recording studio and quickly put four songs down on tape. They came out alright, but we were rushed for time and could not devote enough attention to each song to ensure top quality. I began to focus on more of a final result and asked myself what it would take to record and release an independent album. I had never worked in a recording studio before, and watching the time (and the bill) run up by the minute, I knew we could not afford to go that route.

The goal was still the same: to record an album. We decided to take a chance and build a small recording studio in the garage. We did a little research on the equipment used in such a studio and, with the help of a credit card or two, bought a small recording system. After connecting about a hundred different wires, we powered up the system and began to experiment. We managed to put one song on tape, but it was a disaster. In our excitement, we did just about everything wrong. We recorded the sounds improperly, pressed all the wrong buttons, and in general had no idea what we were doing. We asked a few questions, read a book or two on recording, and tried again. We thought it would take us a month or so "just to learn the equipment." It took us about five months, but we eventually learned how to record properly.

In a recording studio, each instrument is recorded on a separate section of the tape and can be isolated and enhanced. We brought in the rest of the band and recorded the new songs we had written. After that, Tony and I began listening to music that we both liked. We listened for the sound of each instrument and we asked ourselves what the engineer did to get those sounds. Later, we took our tape and began experimenting with each of the recorded tracks, eventually getting them to sound the way we wanted. To us, that meant sounding professional. Once we did that with one song, the rest were easy.

There were many long and cold nights in that garage, and there were times when it seemed like we weren't getting anywhere. The garage was not soundproof, and every barking dog, yelling child, and passing airplane would show up on the tape if we weren't careful. After a year, however, we had twelve final recordings that we were happy with, even though we knew next to nothing about the recording process when we started.

Finished Products

I had a finished book and a finished album "in the can," as they say in the entertainment business, but there were times in each process where I could barely face the tasks of the moment. I kept imagining how happy I'd be the moment I saw the finished product and that's what kept me going. Now comes another challenge. At this point, both *The Ultimate Lesson* and the Veronica's Toy album are about to be manufactured. The next step in both cases is the distribution and promotion process. I don't know much about that part yet...but I will soon.

What's Next For Me?

I enjoy a good challenge, and since a familiar pursuit is rarely challenging, chances are I will throw myself into something I know little or nothing about. If you want to do something, think of a good reason to do it. There are few activities as energizing as pursuing something you enjoy that results in the achievement of a worthy goal. I constantly use all ten points of *The Ultimate Lesson*, as I hope you will in the pursuit of your own goals. You'll seek satisfaction and rewards, you'll face obstacles and confront fears, and you'll be pulled along by your own driving motivation. All great achievements begin with little more than an idea together with a person determined to turn that idea into a reality.

I encourage you to write to me with stories of your own achievements. My address is on the order form in the back of this book. Tell me how little you knew about your subject at the start, tell me what you learned and how you taught yourself. Tell me what motivated you and what obstacles you faced. Most important of all, tell me how you felt the moment you achieved whatever you set out to do.

One last example. As I write this section, I face the challenge of bringing this book to you. As you read this section, you'll know I met that challenge. Does *The Ultimate Lesson* work? You bet it does.

Acknowledgments

I would like to thank the following people:

Cynthia Frank, John Freemont, and Marla Greenway of Cypress House for editing; Robert Kim for my photo; Julia Ryan and Deb Vincent of Dunn & Associates, and Susan Kendrick for advice on the cover; Sara Patton for interior design advice and proofreading; James Wilde, Patricia Coenraad, and Rick Wills of Banta Book Group for the printing.

Order Form

Please send ___ copies of "The Ultimate Lesson" ($14.95) to:

Name: _____

Company Name: _____

Address: _____

City: _____ State: _____ Zip: _____

Sales Tax:
Please add 8.25% for all orders shipped to a California address.

Shipping and Handling:
Book Rate: Please add $2.50 for the first book, $1.00 for each additional book.

Total: $_____

Payment Method: Check ___
                   Visa/MC ___

Card number: _____

Name on Card: _____ Exp. Date: ___ / ___

Signature: _____

Postal Orders: **SLI Press**
                   16161 Ventura Blvd., #C-753
                   Los Angeles, California 91436

World Wide Web: **http://www.selflearn.com**

Comments: _____

_____

_____

_____

_____